Praise for
How Shall I Stand Between River and Land?

In this extraordinary book, Leni de Mik illuminates our understanding of resilience and transformation through her moving reflections on surviving trauma and starvation during World War II, the hardships of immigration, her intellectual and spiritual journey, and wisdom gleaned from decades of practice as a clinical psychologist. Her insights and practical guidance for an authentic and meaningful life harmonize beautifully with decades of research on human resilience.

ANN S. MASTEN   Author of *Ordinary Magic: Resilience in Development,* and Regents Professor Emerita of Child Development at the University of Minnesota

How Shall I Stand Between River and Land? symbolizes the delicate balance we seek amidst the chaos of life. In a world that often feels tumultuous and unpredictable, the quest for self-discovery has never been more essential. This book, amidst the fear of war and economic instability, offers a beacon of hope and a roadmap for personal growth and resilience in these troubled times. Each page challenges you to examine not only your own experiences but also your connection to the world around you. This book beautifully illustrates the intricate weaving of our personal journeys into humanity's larger tapestry, thus making you feel connected and part of something bigger. Let the wisdom of your heart guide you on your next adventure and let this book be your companion on the journey of self-discovery.

SUZIE HOUSLEY   Midwest Book Review

Feeling adrift in an uncertain world? Leni de Mik's *How Shall I Stand Between River and Land?* offers a welcome guide. With wisdom gained from her experience adapting across four cultures, she understands the challenges of change firsthand. Leni helps us find a way to stay true to who we are even when everything around us is shifting. Her stories act as a compass for how to lead with your values and build authentic, trust-based connections. If you're looking for courage, confidence, and balance in our chaotic times, this is a must-read.

ERIN MEYER *New York Times* best-selling author of *No Rules Rules* and *The Culture Map*

This book is amazing! It is part memoir, part psychology, part admonition to the reader—there is so much in it! To me, it represents a lifetime of living, experience, and thought. Simply amazing.

MARILYN J. KAMAN International judge, United Nations mission in Kosovo

Leni de Mik began her life in the Netherlands where her father accepted the dangers of being a leader in the Resistance to Nazi occupation. Dr. de Mik became a psychologist in the United States. This is a journal of her heart's self-discovery. Maturing is not a process of simply coming to understand the world outside. Rather, it is an awakening, a self-exploration, where one becomes brave enough to grow in empathy and arrive at compassion for broadest sense of our shared humanity. Life stories, this story, must be read with intuition, that is between the lines, to appreciate her heart's wisdom.

STEVEN MILES, MD Prof Emeritus of Medicine and Bioethics, University of Minnesota, author of *The Torture Doctors: Human Rights Crimes and the Road to Justice*

As a long-time Buddhist teacher and author, I am happy to say that this is a book that has no "stink of Buddhism" (Leni also has spent years as a Buddhist practitioner) or of any specific religion, which lends to both its value and its deep spirituality. Drawing on her own experience, Leni illustrates the relationship between opening up your heart to a timeless stillness and reaching out and supporting others who are suffering—what the 13th century Zen teacher Dogen called, forgetting the self and acting from a feeling of "intimacy with all life." Leni serves as a role model for us all in her ability to do this.

TIM BURKETT Author of *Nothing Holy About It, Zen in the Age of Anxiety*, and *Enlightenment Is an Accident*

Weaving together wisdom, experience, and life stories, Leni de Milk has created a tapestry for living a heart-centered life. Blending practical guidance and thoughtful reflections, *How Shall I Stand Between River & Land?* offers inspiration for those seeking a balance between personal growth and a purposeful relationship with the world around them.

HELEN DAVIDSON Blogger and life-story facilitator for older women at agelesspossibilities.org

The world is crying out for wise elders to step forward in these troubling times. Leni de Mik's new book is a clarion call to return to our hearts in a world gone mad. We all benefit from her 80+ years of experience and wisdom as she chronicles a life of activism in service to life. Read it now!

PATRICIA AND CRAIG NEAL Past publisher of *Utne Reader*, and co-founders, Center for Purposeful Leadership, co-authors, *The Art of Convening*

It is a terrible loss to define ourselves as victims of trauma and grieve the collapse of our easy way of life. Leni's book shines with the clear light of wisdom gained from fully living life no matter its harshness. Here, we learn questions and practices to awaken the power of the heart, no longer diminished as victims, people engaging wholeheartedly with life as caring and confident contributors. Thank you Leni.

MARGARET WHEATLEY   Author of 13 books, from *Leadership and The New Science* to *Restoring Sanity*

How Shall I Stand
Between River & Land?

How
Shall
I Stand
Between
River &
Land?

HEART QUESTIONS FOR
UNCERTAIN TIMES

Leni de Mik, PhD

With a Foreword
by Parker J. Palmer

CREATIVE
COURAGE
PRESS

Creative Courage Press, LLC (Palisade, CO)
www.CreativeCouragePress.com

ISBN 978-1-959921-080 (paperback)
ISBN 978-1-959921-097 (ebook)

First edition (all formats): 2025

Library of Congress Cataloging-in-Publication Data
Names: Mik, Leni de, author. | Palmer, Parker J., foreword author.
Title: How shall I stand between river and land? Heart questions for uncertain times / by Leni de Mik, PhD; with a foreword by Parker J. Palmer.
Description: Includes bibliographical references. | Palisade, CO: Creative Courage Press, 2025.
Identifiers: LCCN: 2025913517| ISBN: 9781959921080 (print) | 9781959921097 (ebook) Subjects: LCSH Psychologists—United States—Biography. | Intuition. | Self help. | Self-realization. | Self-actualization (Psychology) | BISAC SELF-HELP / Motivational & Inspirational | BIOGRAPHY & AUTOBIOGRAPHY / Memoirs | PSYCHOLOGY / Emotions
Classification: LCC BJ1470 .M55 2025 | DDC 158.1—dc23

Cover and interior design: KP Books

Cover painting: Leni de Mik
Editor: Shelly Francis
Proofreader: Rebecca K. Job
Author photo courtesy of author

Contents

Foreword

Parker J. Palmer

Author of *Let Your Life Speak*, *A Hidden Wholeness*, *Healing the Heart of Democracy*, and *On the Brink of Everything*

———

THIS BOOK SEEKS to answer an age-old question: Where can we go for guidance, inspiration, and the courage to act wisely, especially in morally challenging times? The question has been with us forever, but rarely has it been more pressing than it is today in the midst of our global calamity.

For Leni de Mik, the answer is clear. Beneath all of life's complexities and confusions lies the wisdom of the heart, that deep core of the human self where all of our faculties for knowing ourselves and the world converge. The heart does not shout at us but speaks softly. It does not issue marching orders but often speaks first as a question that requires us to go inward toward a quiet place where the racket of fear, confusion, and discord are silenced, and we have a chance to listen for an answer. When we have the patience required to follow that question and dwell in that silence, the wisdom of the heart can be heard. The question then becomes, will we follow its lead?

Leni de Mik's wise counsel comes not from the intellect alone but from life experience. Born to Dutch parents in 1941 during the Nazi occupation of the Netherlands—another era of global calamity—shaped by her father's role in the Resistance, her emigration to Canada, her decades as a U.S.

citizen, and her work as a clinical psychologist, Leni brings it all together here in a book that is timely, inspirational, and practical.

Using parables, ancient wisdom and modern science, client stories, and her own life experiences, she proposes ways we can foster hope, generate solutions, and weave life-sustaining connections through small, daily opportunities: with a gesture of gratitude, a hand on a shoulder, a word of encouragement, or a smile and a nod. Even when illness or age become confining, we can continue to make a difference. As the poet John Milton wrote, "They also serve, who only stand and wait."

From her experience in World War II and again during the COVID-19 pandemic, Leni learned that it defies the nature of our interconnected existence to sit by and do nothing, paralyzed by fear, while others are endangered. Now as then, withdrawal, avoidance, and retreat into individualism will not solve the challenges of our times, nor will they sustain our hearts and souls. For Leni, as for her father in the Resistance, it boils down to "heart questions" that must be met with awareness, with answers, with choices, with words and actions and ways of life.

Leni reminds us that we are not powerless. We can choose connection over isolation, seek out and listen to diverse voices and conversations, and build bridges to understanding. We can choose action, support efforts already under way. By taking small steps in shared humanity and on common ground, we can turn fear into resolve, division into collaboration, and uncertainty into a shared journey. Together, we are stronger, more effective, and more resilient than we can ever be alone.

But to be available to others, we must do the inner work necessary to make ourselves available to ourselves. As Leni writes, "When we tend to our physical, emotional, and spiritual needs, we become better equipped to serve others authentically and sustainably, transforming our individual pursuits into a collective endeavor of caring for all beings." We must rescue our hearts from all that holds them captive, including the many fears that lead us to "play it safe" and avoid taking risks in service of others. From the deep and rich life experience chronicled in this book, Leni offers many responses to the question, "How shall we follow, fortify, and open our hearts in these uncertain times?"

From childhood onward, Leni de Mik has understood that connection, relationship, and community are the keys to the fullness of human life, the source of shared joy in good times and shared sustenance in hard times. So it is more than incidental that this book—this plea for the kind of inner work that leads us to care for each other and the common good—is itself the direct result of a profound friendship that Leni had with another great soul of our time, a woman whom I too had the privilege of knowing.

Leni met Joyce McFarland some thirty years ago, and Joyce introduced me to Leni about six years ago. As Leni says in an epilogue to this book, Joyce was a "master connector." It was as if she had been born with an ability to spot human need, to spot the gifts of people who might serve those needs, to encouraging them individually, and when needed, to bring them together in service of the common good.

Born into a family with an instinct for public service and the resources to help, Joyce married Dick McFarland, whose commitment to public service matched her own. Together they formed the McFarland Family Foundation, which to this day continues to serve the great cause of love, truth, and justice.

When Joyce and Leni met, they quickly recognized each other as soul sisters, both of them as deeply devoted to the inner work that grounds us as to the outer work that serves the world's needs. Joyce was eager to make sure that the larger world had a chance to learn Leni's story and benefit from Leni's wisdom, so when she died in May 2022, Joyce left a bequest in support of this book. Leni, for her part, was equally eager to do the hard work required to honor and keep Joyce's spirit alive with a book that responds to the ancient question, "How, then, shall we live?"

From Aristotle to C.S. Lewis to Rebecca Solnit, from Buddhism to Christianity, friendship has been regarded as one of the keys to living a virtuous life. The book you hold in your hands is the result of the kind of friendship that, multiplied many times over, could save the world.

Questions of Becoming

From where I stand I cannot see how the river began
or when it will fall finally into something else.

Ziggy Rendler-Bregman, poet and artist

———

I RECALL ASKING myself a question when I was 10 years old. *What happened the day I was born?* The answer was no surprise. I already knew it but wanted to hear again my mother's quiet response: "I gave birth to you at home; Nazis patrolled the streets. The sky was black with planes, their bellies filled with bombs."

I was in the womb when the Nazi army crossed the border and occupied our small village in the western Netherlands, in the province of South Holland where my family had lived for countless generations. If you look at a map, you can see how close we were to the North Sea and on to England. Also, why we were in the path of bombs coming from Allied places and headed to Germany. I was born in August 1941.

For five years, the village was occupied, and German and British bombers darkened the skies. The Battle of the Bulge and Operation Market Garden were so close we had to evacuate as the front approached. During the war, Holland's economy collapsed. My father's family construction business building roads and dikes was destroyed. In retaliation for assisting the Allies, the Nazis had blocked food supplies to Western Holland in November 1944. We were plunged into famine. It was winter, the coldest winter in Dutch history;

more than 20,000 people in our small province died of starvation as temperatures plummeted into the unholy cold. After the war, the country was in ruins, and Stalin was rising and looming in the East. But we were still behind enemy lines many months after some of Holland was free.

I knew of and was deeply influenced by my father's participation in the Dutch Resistance of World War II. After the war, he served on a town council to reconstruct the village and was responsible for holding villagers accountable for Nazi collaboration. Villagers at that time were publicly acclaimed and censured. Choices had been made. In the terror of being hunted, of death by starvation, some had collaborated. Others, like my father, had resisted and risked their lives in service.

My family and an estimated 8 million other Europeans were part of a fear-filled, hope-filled, post-war exodus. To find a better future, we emigrated. Finding a new home was a kind of lottery. Where you landed depended on which country would accept you. Many who left our village ended up in Brazil or South Africa. By chance, we found a sponsor in Canada. The childhood years of war passed; life went on.

When I was 18, I went to Calvin, a Christian college in Michigan, married an American, and became a U.S. citizen. A few years later, to pursue my then-husband's postdoctoral work in physics, we moved to Munich, once the home and heart of Hitler's regime. In a strange twist of fate, I found myself living with Germans again. This time, we met in peace. It turned out to be a profound gift. This time, I learned about the war and its aftermath from a new perspective, from their lived experience. It was a period of deep reflection and change for me.

Questions have marked my life. "What did you do during the war?" "What will I do when I'm afraid like that? When the risk is high?" Questions about accountability for choices have been with me since childhood—questions like *why am I here?* and *what is my responsibility at this moment?* Questions like this are not new to me; such questions of purpose and meaning have been woven through my life.

Perhaps because of the immediacy of those early questions, I became an activist in our life that followed the war and migration. My questioning never ceased. Questions informed my life choices as I went from being a teacher in Appalachia, an administrator of an Experimental College at the University of Minnesota, a hospice planner, an anti-war protester, a civil and human rights activist, and finally, a clinical psychologist. Along the way, I became a multi-lingual citizen of three countries and a resident of four.

As a clinical psychologist for 40-plus years, I'm familiar with trauma. I have given lectures about surviving adversity, led therapy groups for those with PTSD, and volunteered for disaster relief. I've welcomed refugees into my home. Even so, I learned some of the most ground- and gut-level knowledge of life in my first decade, during the years of war, reconstruction, and immigration.

Eighty-plus years later, I recognize the early exposure to hunger, war, and death as doorways. Traces of war remain in my bones, in my DNA, in my patterns of arousal, in the texture of my relationships, and in my heart. Like improbable teachers, they continue to inform and enrich me as I grow older, revealing insights and veiled truths I might never have chosen to know. But I needed to learn the power of reflection, of asking hard "heart questions" and sitting without answers until they eventually arose within me.

Today, my childhood might receive the label of trauma, but I cringe at the label. Few Europeans I knew as a child characterized it that way. Instead, it was war, the life lived by everyone. Not everyone turns an eye back on their life to unravel its meaning.

Trauma is often seen through a lens that considers its harm, damage, and healing. I'm not sure how that fits for me. If being shielded from grief and pain is good, then so be it. Writers, Hemingway among them, suggest that harrowing experiences hold opportunity, that broken places can knit together in new ways that strengthen us, sharpen our sense of purpose, and enhance our process of finding meaning. Given the choice, I would not exchange my childhood for a childhood of comfort and safety.

As the youngest, I was cared for by protective parents and seven older siblings (who, like a trained chorus, would snatch me up, throw me in a washtub, and run for the bomb shelter when sirens wailed). I now believe it possible that early-life war experience and exposure to danger may have infused me with a "felt sense," a mixture of uncertainty intertwined with an inner assurance of safety in danger. Perhaps the call to challenging circumstances that I later felt stemmed from a need to prove that I was brave and unafraid.

As an adult, I was curiously drawn to (and subsequently traveled to) places that deterred others—risky places where war, devastation, violence, or authoritarianism was a way of life. Such places attracted and scared me but did not deter me. In later years, my psychologist-trained mind tried to puzzle it out (as did my heart). What inner voice was beckoning? Was I unconsciously drawn to return to an earlier atmosphere of

HOW SHALL I STAND BETWEEN RIVER & LAND?

uncertainty and tension? Was it a call to return, to taste once more of early experiences I did not fully understand?

I think of my childhood as a mix of gifts and wounds. It was a lived experience that instilled an expanded foundation of "knowing." The exposure to and familiarity with hardship and uncertainty cultivated resilience. I could not have come by these facets of my identity in any other way. They have called me to activism and instilled a desire to serve; they have served me well.

AND THEN CAME COVID

For many years, I had not thought much about my early days. That changed in 2020 when COVID-19 arrived, along with new questions for my heart.

Like other introverts, I enjoyed life during the pandemic at times. COVID offered a reprieve from small talk and extroverted social responsibilities that can quickly exhaust me. But it also removed the opportunity for the warm exchanges and deep conversations I typically welcome. As time passed, I felt not particularly afraid of the virus itself; I practiced safety, showed up for vaccinations, and faithfully wore masks.

As I saw it, during COVID, as during the war, we lived with a common threat. Some of us were protected and served by essential workers risking their lives and the well-being of their families. Some of us lived in danger of isolation and despair, in fear of compromising the immune system. Some reached out to touch, to be with others. Some withdrew into silos of personal safety. ○

However, I also saw that life seemed desperate for others. When I checked in with friends, online or outside, I felt a charge; I sensed their bodies contracting against a looming specter of imminent danger. And this broad-based fear also had an impact on me. I slipped through and back in time, found myself suddenly reliving the days of my childhood and harkening to a sometimes-painful flood of memories.

I was not the only one so troubled. As the virus spread and deaths piled up, Nelly, my remaining sibling, who is 10 years older and a widow, called from Michigan. She was in lockdown, and she, too, was now often reliving the past.

Nelly explained how she was glued to the news and having nightmares. To my surprise, her dreams were two-natured. She was responding to COVID media news and pandemic safety restrictions, but even more prominently to deeper, older fears. She explained how she was being triggered by President Trump, for whom she had voted.

This fact astonished me. I listened. My sister described reliving the political tension of the 1930s when Hitler's power was gathering. She expressed her dismay and how she felt alone in her fear. "They don't get it," she said, "They did not live it," referring to her Michigan family and neighbors. I understood. I knew. I felt it as well.

Today, few remain to carry the lived experience of World War II, of life in the direct path of a storm that would cost millions of lives and would spur mass migration. Like my sister, what I remembered from childhood impacted my perception of life during the pandemic.

I toggled between WWII and COVID, remembering how isolation had been checked by the rules of the Geneva Convention and wondering what the resisters of World War II would have done in the circumstances presented by COVID. If isolation was not okay then, could it be all right now? How does history affect our moral compass, choices, and decisions?

I felt the shadow of war; I felt alone. Others did not seem to feel the weight of my perceptual filter. Some would call it trauma or unhealed wounding; it did not feel like a wound.

I think of it as "conditioned attunement," the legacy of lived experience.

Today, no longer in the extremes of COVID, we are facing the rise of fascism, authoritarian regimes, and an existential threat to democracy not only in the United States but globally. Questions of choice arise every moment as we target care, extending to self, family, community, or all of these. Our moral core, this true north, is present not only in our larger actions. It manifests in the smallest genuine gestures: a gentle touch, a word of encouragement, a helping hand. Big things are made up of small things, and small things cultivate big things. The potency of humble dailiness is at the heart of our democracy.

As my life nears its natural transition, I think about the future of the children about to embark on their journey on our amazing, life-giving planet. I remember how global wars in the past century left an estimated 100 million dead. I feel the tearing of the earth's fabric, the Anthropocene. I wonder about climate change.

It's hard not to worry about the children. I remember how hunger and survival drive mass migration. We recently had the first Minnesota winter without winter. There are daily reports of catastrophic weather conditions.

When will we start to beg for water? I won't be here, but other generations will reap the harvest of our choices. How will they live? How will they survive?

I reflect on these future possibilities, aware of the darkness of my war-shaped view of life—sometimes an uncomfortable, unshared experience. How can you imagine or feel the impact of what you have not experienced?

Questions for our head demand immediate answers, but questions for the heart require more patience. Questions can raise awareness of the choices before us, sharpening the blade of discernment and encouraging the unconscious to become conscious. Practice makes it possible to seek answers from our heart, for our heart. We can then see more clearly where we can choose to reach out or hold back. We know the price and reward of choices more clearly as we decide whether to call a "needy" friend, go for a run, read a book, or visit a neighbor in an assisted living facility. As we make choices, we are transmuted. Each action is revealed as a choice of targeted awareness, care, and expression of what matters at that moment.

As we practice asking heart questions and seeking our truest answers, we come to know ourselves. We learn to be aware of our choices and consequences. We gain direct insight into how we balance our internal hierarchy of values. We might witness what is for us "object, other, or thing" (as religious thinker Martin Buber coined it), and what we designate sacred, "Thou."

Even today, many suffer from things that we cannot even imagine. Like all things, moral fortitude thrives when cultivated—in part with good questions. There will always be heroes who will lead with unwavering courage and love. We don't have to be heroes, but we can do small things, be good to each other, and care about the common good.

RIPPLES OF AWARENESS

When we are completely at ease with our own being,
the ripples of awareness naturally spread out in all
directions, touching the lives of everyone we meet.

Yongey Mingyur Rinpoche

Many of us can't imagine what it would feel like to be "completely at ease with our own being." Few of us are fully confident about our ability to nurture deep, meaningful, empowering connections with people inside and outside our family and social circles. How can we cultivate the self-awareness necessary for self-compassion, much less compassion for others and finding common ground? This is one of the most important heart questions we must consider today.

We are at a crossroads, divided along economic, social, political, and religious lines; we live in a time where divisions threaten to harden. As we turn on the news, we witness political distrust, mass migrations, extinctions, and war. We experience unusual, disturbing changes in local weather patterns. The future can seem dark, shrouded in uncertainty as we look ahead. Fear and overwhelm can paralyze us. Resistance can seem futile.

As we look for a way forward, we can ask many questions, most without clear, certain answers: How do we move beyond divisions? How shall we respond to these local and global challenges? What can we do, what *must* we do, to be part of the solution, to ensure a safe, sustainable world for future generations, for our kids and grandkids? How can we restore a harmonious, respectful relationship with our planet?

Part One of this book, "Embracing the Mystery and Complexity of the Heart," focuses on the self, the inner life where the heart's journey to wholeness and authenticity begins. It calls attention to the obstacles, challenges, and choices readers will be asked to consider. It suggests provisions that may be needed to sustain the resolution to stay on the heart path. I have walked this path alone and with others. I hope to provide guidance as you navigate the journey's weeds, snags, and pitfalls.

Part Two, "Reclaiming the Heart, Again and Again," is where our orientation shifts from "me" to "we." Here, the heart journey begins in earnest. It's where, over and over, we recognize that our circle of care is too narrow, our sense of belonging too thin, and our social structure too fragile. To reclaim the heart again and again, we must find the courage to stand alone when necessary, the wisdom to connect when possible, and the resolve to take the next step—sometimes alone, sometimes with the support of others.

Part Three, "Alchemy of an Undivided Heart," is where the small *we*, born of limited compassion, becomes the big *WE*, and we begin to realize what it means to live and act in an interconnected universe. The wisdom of WE is not new.

Each chapter ends with heart questions for your own reflection.

Ultimately, this book seeks to answer the question: Where can we go for direction, inspiration, and courage to act wisely? For me, the unfailing source found beneath all superficial, judgmental, fear-based, discriminative discourse is the self-aware wisdom of the heart. This wisdom often begins as a question that draws us inward toward a quiet place where the voices of fear, confusion, and discord are stilled. There, the heart speaks.

PART I

Embracing the Mystery and Complexity of the Heart

We awaken by asking the right questions.

Suzy Kassem

Chapter 1

Your Heart Is Your Greatest Untapped Power

The heart has reasons that reason cannot know.

Blaise Pascal

———

FOR MOST OF us, the questions that keep us up at night have to do with job security, concern for family, our possessions, how to get what we want or pay for what we have, our status, the size of our paycheck, the promotion we deserve, and the raise that comes with it.

We question decisions we made in the past and what our future may look like. We relive our mistakes over and over. The questions we focus on weigh heavily during our waking hours and haunt our dreams at night.

This is no accident. We've been conditioned since childhood to measure our worth by the responses we receive from our communities. Our self-esteem hangs on how the world sees us.

At times, we drift. Life becomes prescribed, dull, and colorless as we mindlessly become prisoners of our striving. It happens over time, over years of worry, as failures and successes come and go, leaving us numb. We often don't know when it happened or how we became prisoners of routine, automatons moving through the well-trodden ruts of our lives.

And yet, all it can take to shift is one small crack in the armor around our hearts. It might be a heart-stopping phone call, or that one visit to the doctor's office where a dreaded diagnosis is confirmed, or the day of that abrupt dismissal and termination from a job. Just enough for the thinnest shaft of light to enter and awaken us to the realization that the approval of others and the accumulation of things don't amount to a hill of beans.

Perhaps a tiny crack that allows the light in can remind us that what really matters is our capacity for love and courage, our ability to feel rather than react, and our connection with others as givers and receivers of compassion. This dawning awareness can help us commit to hearing the quiet voice that tells us who we are, opening the door to a well-lived life.

I invite you to ponder the questions that matter, that can make a difference in our lives and maybe even our world. Questions that nurture our inner life and infuse our simplest moments with meaning. These are the questions of an awakening heart, and they are infused with wisdom, courage, and your greatest untapped power.

A MOMENT OF AWAKENING ON MY HEART'S PATH

Growing up, I was no stranger to independence and self-reliance. My childhood after immigration was marked by a double-edged autonomy. Today, it might be called benign neglect. I had learned early on to navigate life's challenges alone, often without guidance. There was no other way. It was unremarkable; it was simply how life was for everyone. But I found an unseen benefit; unsupervised, I could do what I wanted without risk of discovery. My childhood was marked by a quiet rebellion, sometimes a sneaky and secretive defiance against the Dutch values in my home and the limitations imposed on me. I never asked; I just did. Whether it was signing my own report cards or writing notes to my teachers that my mother signed without knowing what I had written. My individual experiences were lost in the ongoing crisis as each family member tried to find a way to adjust and survive. What I did was rarely shared or acknowledged. I learned not to expect that.

As a child I asked, *Who am I? Why am I here?* I asked myself that frequently, concluding that I was here merely because my parents had decided to have sex. I would just as soon not have been here (today, I would have been diagnosed with early childhood pervasive depression). As a teen, my heart questions became, *Who can I be? Where am I going? What do I want?*

Yet I never gave much thought to college. It was not a familiar topic nor a conversation in the family. In Ontario, school attendance was mandatory until age 16, or grade 12, when there was a set of government exams. (Canada was too poor for publicly funded universities; there were only five in Ontario in the 1950s). I sat for those exams, and my score gave me entry to grade 13 (the equivalent of freshman year in college—university was three years).

When the university door opened, it seemed way beyond my reach—but, perhaps for the first time, I started to think about a personal future. Personal futures were a low family priority. Everyone was still trying to dig themselves out of the financial pit of my mother's health. My sister Betsy was in a mental hospital. The mortgage had to be paid, and whoever could work, worked.

I had luck. I was in a catechism class led by Reverend Van Kooten. For some reason, he saw something in me that perhaps even I did not fully recognize—a potential that deserved to be nurtured. He spoke with my parents when he came for a family spiritual visit, a *huis besoek*. He suggested that my gifts were worth developing. He told them about a Christian college in Grand Rapids, Michigan.

Calvin College would be a place where I could be educated without compromising the Calvinist faith they held dear. He encouraged them to let me go, to allow me to be educated and use my brain, to discover a different way to be in the world, and to step out of the working class that immigration had plunged us into. His empathy for me and my parents was life-changing, setting me on a new track that would define the rest of my life.

My parents felt assured that I would not turn into a heathen there. For them, it was something like, "Why not? She will earn her way; she needs to find a path. Let's do it, let's let her go!"

My decision to attend Calvin College was fraught with fear and apprehension; it was an opportunity my siblings had not had. I did not yet know that I was smart and thought I did well only because I was an overachiever and worked so hard. Leaving Canada to live in the United States felt like a daunting leap into the unknown. I knew I would be on my own, working to support myself and earning the finances necessary to stay in school. The connections and conveniences we take for granted today simply did not exist; I would not have auto transportation, and the cost of phone calls meant limited communication with my family. The thought of returning home only a few times a year was both liberating and terrifying. Yet, something deeper than fear drove me to take the risk—perhaps it was a longing for independence, a cry for freedom, or even an emerging sense of self-love. I love my family and know they loved me, but it was not hard to leave. The decision to go was a heart choice, a risk worth taking. At almost 18, off I went.

At Calvin College, I encountered ideas and perspectives that shattered the narrow confines of my previous understanding. I studied history, archeology, literature, philosophy, and art history. I was expanding my exposure and being changed by what I learned. I was on a path of pursuing the true, the good, and the beautiful.

One college class transformed me, this time at the University of Ohio where I finished by undergraduate degree. It was my first philosophy of religion class, where the air was thick with intellectual curiosity. The professor, Dr. Stanley Greon, was a Presbyterian minister whose teachings opened an entirely new world for me. He introduced us to thinkers and concepts I had never imagined: Paul Tillich (a profoundly subtle theologian who put *doubt* at the center of his thought), Martin Buber, Thomas Merton, and even the Dhammapada, a slim Buddhist volume that has remained with me all my life.

It was a revelation.

In that classroom, under Dr. Greon's guidance, I began to see the world through a different lens. Learning became more than just the accumulation of knowledge; it became an ongoing journey of self-discovery. I started to question, to challenge, and to explore uncharted territories of thought. My mind expanded beyond Calvinism, beyond the limitations I had previously accepted.

Dr. Greon's class validated many questions I had but could not discuss with my family. I had been scripted to believe that everything in the Bible was literally accurate. I could respect it as a metaphor, but this made no sense. The difference was an area of no discussion. Since the Bible was divinely inspired, every word in it was accurate. But unlike for others in my family, the Bible didn't answer my questions, and they kept coming. What is true? What do I believe? How do I understand reality? Not only those existential questions, but also: What is freedom? Responsibility? God's purpose? How do I make sense of the war, of death by torture, of my sister suffering in a provincial insane asylum like *One Flew Over the Cuckoo's Nest*? How could I make meaning of my mother's depression, her loneliness, and what I knew about the torture of people in concentration camps?

These questions were spoken to, and I finally found people asking similar questions. Suddenly, my questions were validated! I breathed more easily. I was no longer alone.

Dr. Greon opened a landscape where I felt hope—a green branch, long dormant, unfurling within me. Suddenly, the boundaries around my understanding dissolved. Ideas I could safely explore swung open to a new way of seeing the world. I felt a validation for my quest! I was in heaven.

Dr. Greon's philosophy class was a turning point. It awakened in me an awareness that transformed my understanding of the world and my place in it. He made a crucial distinction between cultural mores and moral beliefs, a difference that rippled out into my life and later served me well as a clinical psychologist. This distinction clarified the chaos in my mind and allowed me to align my deepest feelings with a newfound sense of resolve in my heart.

The journey was risky. In my community, obedience to tradition trumped questioning. I held my silence, unwilling to face the resistance and rejection I anticipated would arise if I dared to speak. It solidified a pattern of privacy, of keeping what I believe to myself. But the seeds of change had been planted, and there was no turning back.

Thanks to Dr. Greon, I found a path—a road that led me away from the darkness of spiritual disillusionment and into the light of intellectual and spiritual exploration. He opened doors I never knew existed and gave me the courage to walk through them. It was like T.S. Eliot's description of being "pierced by joy," a profound glimpse of something greater than myself, something that would guide me for the rest of my life.

This is one moment / But know that another /
shall pierce you with a sudden painful joy.

T.S. Eliot

AN AWAKENING HEART IS A RESPONSIVE HEART

The heart is intricately connected to our emotional state. When we experience joy, compassion, or empathy, our hearts beat harmoniously, fostering a sense of calm and contentment. The experience of stress, anger, and negative emotions can disrupt this rhythm, evidencing the interplay between our emotional well-being and the heart's physical health.

Deeper still, the heart is central to intuitive intelligence. Recent scientific research suggests that the heart contains a complex network of neurons similar to the brain's. This network allows the heart to process information and communicate with the brain in ways previously unrecognized. That means the heart may profoundly influence decision-making, problem-solving, and overall cognitive function.

Moreover, heart-centered emotions enhance the brain's ability to regulate bodily functions. For example, you can improve your immune system by conjuring positive emotions, whereas negative emotions can wreak havoc on the nervous system and body.

While science tells us that emotions impact our bodies, we aren't always conscious of their impact; it takes awareness. If aware, we can experience the relationship between heart-based feelings and our physical well-being. We might find that gratitude provides better sleep, improves mood, and boosts our immune system. Compassion leads to better mental outcomes; kindness increases a sense of belonging and reduction of social isolation. The heart's capacity for empathy, to understand the experiences and emotions of others, provides the underlying bond of connectedness we experience in relationships. Heart choices allow us to live authentic lives, to reach out to others from the center of our being, and to forge our place in the web of human communities.

And yet, questions remain. Do we all feel the same feelings? Do some feelings come into maturity as we mature? Do we *grow into* gratitude, kindness, empathy, connectedness, and belonging? Are they amplified or subdued by our environment? Gratitude, kindness, etc. are all great, but life demands more. It takes asking, "What is true for me? What values do I live by?" And answering those questions takes courage.

FIND YOUR HEART, FIND YOUR COURAGE

Courage is the most important of all the
virtues because without courage, you can't
practice any other virtue consistently.

Maya Angelou

Have you ever felt stuck, perhaps in a life that wasn't the one you dreamed of? On the path of self-discovery, getting stuck is par for the course. *Stuck* in a place of significant discomfort, where the status quo clings to us like glue; where our heart yearns for change, but we feel immovable. When we're stopped in our tracks and can't take another step or even see beyond our feet, that is often the birthplace of transformational change.

Getting unstuck is not an external endeavor; it's an internal one. It demands a deep excavation, an unearthing of our fears, and a confrontation with our resistance. Rumi tells us, "The cure for the pain is in the pain." This paradoxical wisdom underscores the importance of turning inward to find the courage required for transformation.

Getting unstuck often begins with recognizing that fear is our most formidable adversary. Fear can paralyze, hold us hostage to the familiar, and prevent us from embracing change. It can convince us that the risks of change outweigh the rewards. Fear can tell us we are not responsible for being stuck, a victim without agency to create change in our lives.

Heart wisdom knows otherwise: it sees how denying our authentic selves the opportunity to flourish is the greatest risk!

It takes courage to take that impossible first step, face our fears head-on, acknowledge them without judgment, harness our energy for growth, and break free—but how do we do it? Where will this courage come from?

The path to courage is the inner path of self-awareness. This path calls for self-compassion, an often-overlooked aspect of personal transformation. We must summon the same caring compassion for ourselves as we would for a close friend. We must recognize that we are not alone in humanity's struggles and that we share the common human condition of fear and vulnerability.

The inner path to awareness and courage is a path of self-discovery. On this inward journey, we revisit old stories and review the narratives we live by. We find installed stories, often born of culture, family narratives, and early life experiences. We see how they create patterns that repeat. Awakened awareness provides new views, allowing us to retain, revise, refresh, update, and enrich ourselves with newfound wisdom and understanding. A road to new possibilities greets us as we take the first steps.

At times, we dare to go deeper. Now, we find the courage and self-esteem to face our inner vulnerability, as when I risked leaving my family in Canada to attend college in the

United States. At daring times like this, we uncover another layer of our true selves: not only the good but also the bad. Not only the altruistic but also the selfish, the responsible as well as the irresponsible. Here, we begin to discover and create a means for genuine, authentic self-acceptance of who we are, *just as we are*. We find a new capacity to hold the tension of opposites to shift out of primitive dualities: good or bad, success or failure, adequate or inadequate, loving or mean, kind or unkind. We replace "either-or" dualities with "both-and" and self-acceptance. Resilience strengthens us as we claim ourselves. Unconditional acceptance of and compassion for who we are becomes the foundation for responsibility and accountability.

Both stuck and unstuck lose their grasp as we recognize that, like all things, we are beings shaped in an ongoing process of formation and transformation, ever-evolving and changing.

FIND YOUR HEART, FIND YOUR WISDOM

Traditional wisdom relies on reason, analysis, structured thought processes, and adherence to established principles. Our accumulated knowledge and established cultural, religious, and philosophical systems often shape it, and conclusions and guidance are passed down through generations. Today, much of what we consider true (and wise) is derived from science. As a clinical psychologist, I was trained in the scientific method. I respect and value evidence-based information and critical thinking. I respect scientific openness to advancement and change in how we know. But like experienced carpenters, we need informed tool chests: diverse and different tools for different tasks. Scientific reasoning is insufficient for some things. It cannot access the subtle world below what can be materially measured. This is the realm of heart wisdom.

Heart wisdom requires a worldview not created or solely limited by conditioned beliefs, cultural values, or thought processes from generations past. The heart intuitively understands that we live in the "now" of time, a thoroughly interconnected universe where everything is the cause of everything else, and everything is the effect of everything else. That means we are at times more limited by the world we don't see than by the one we see.

What we don't see, don't think, don't feel, don't believe, and don't know defines our worldview by omission. Our worldview shapes our life and our moment-to-moment experience of being alive. It defines the contours of our happiness and our sadness. It colors every thought we think, and flavors every emotion that arises within us. Our worldview tells us who we may befriend and who we may not. It blinds us to our weaknesses and gives shape to our fear.

Our worldview is like a cup we pour ourselves into. It contains us, shapes us; we feel safe, stable, unchanging, even permanent—so long as the cup is upright, with no cracks, and rests on a level, unmovable surface. But life isn't like that.

What new thoughts might infuse the mind if the cup containing us suddenly shattered and spilled us out into the world? How might the view change if the transcendent emotions of awe, gratitude, and unconditional compassion suddenly began to flood awareness? Can you imagine being so open and unhindered that the energies of aliveness flowed through like the tides, bringing sensations, emotions, and ideas that simultaneously felt strange and familiar?

Might we experience fear and courage at the same time? If all the pathways within suddenly opened up, might it be possible to feel sadness and joy simultaneously? Could we hold the world's weight on our shoulders and simultaneously feel the lightness of just being? Or experience deep grief over the loss of a loved one, and at the same time, grateful for having known them at all?

These are not linear questions that can be figured out with the brain; they are not meant to be puzzles for the intellect. The intellect's skill is superior, unmatched in studying the world we think of as "it," the world of constructs, things, and objects. Heart questions are not static things; they are meant to be lived. Heart questions are invitations to explore the depths of our emotions, values, and purpose, to expand our connection to consciousness. They include a world beyond the one we see. Heart questions open the doorway to something I referred to earlier, what Buber calls the sacred connection, the "Thou" in us, each other, in life itself (for more on this concept, see chapter 6).

Heart questions arise and unfold in their own way and time. Our part is cultivating the capacity and willingness to hold a heart question without seeking the answer—to trust that the questions will open our minds to the mysteries and paradoxes of an expanded consciousness.

Heart questions direct us inward, guiding us along a journey of self-discovery and inner truth. The heart is the dwelling place of our deepest insights and innermost passions. When we're attuned to the heart's questions, we resonate with the world around us, with humanity.

We know this; we recognize the truth of it.

Even so, over and over, we get reeled back in like a fish on a hook by a culture that celebrates the intellect over the quiet wisdom of the heart, prioritizes logic over intuition, analysis over empathy, and too often leaves the heart overshadowed and underestimated. We need both. Both serve us. When the heart and reason come together as "heart-mind," we live in a knowing and understanding of life as a harmonious whole.

FIND YOUR HEART, FIND YOUR POWER

Our heart is what today might be called our "superpower," capable of love, compassion, and resilience. It can be a driving force for the common good. One of the most empowering aspects of the human heart is its capacity for love.

Love is not merely a fleeting emotion; it is a force. Love is like the force and flow of a river; it has been poetically described as a river that carries us, a river that we decide to step away from at our peril. Love can transform lives and shape the course of history. Love—whether it's love for family, friends, or strangers, for non-human animals, nature, art, or all creation—all love has the power to heal, inspire, and unite. Fiercely vulnerable, love motivates acts of kindness, selflessness, and empathy. Leading with our heart empowers us to forge deep connections with others, nature, and the world beyond our immediate experience.

Self-love (sometimes confused with arrogance, self-absorption, and narcissism) is an often-overlooked aspect of the heart's power. Self-love is essential for personal growth and well-being. When we love and accept ourselves, we become more resilient in the face of adversity, better equipped to navigate life's complexities, and more capable of pursuing our dreams.

History is filled with examples of individuals who, led by their hearts, have sparked movements for justice, equality, and peace. From Mahatma Gandhi's nonviolent resistance to Rosa Parks' refusal to give up her bus seat, from Alexei Navalny's return to Russia knowing he'd die to Senator Cory Booker's 25-hour oration, these individuals harnessed the power of their hearts to challenge injustice and inspire transformative change.

The heart's superpower lies not only in its individual potential but also in its ability to connect with and influence the hearts of others. Like a pebble thrown into a pond, it can create a ripple effect, spread outward, and empower everyone in its wake.

HEART CHOICES

As we live, the heart is tested. Life brings choices. Heart choices reveal what really matters on an everyday level. Heart choices can be deceptively simple: Will I give up a favorite program or pastime to help a friend or to visit someone in isolation? Will I stay or go?

As a clinician, I often sat with people stuck in a marriage, a job, or a relationship dilemma. Usually, these circumstances require making a heart (and hard) choice. The choice frequently comes with questions: What if I make the wrong choice? What if I live to regret it? How do I know what is the best option?

The answer is often a leap of faith: Do your best, draw on your resources, and risk the unknown. Some of us eventually decide the unknown is preferable to the known. The poet John O'Donohue told of learning "to find ease in risk."[1] But where do we find such ease?

While some heart choices are seemingly insignificant, others, like "Sophie's choice,"[2] bring heartache beyond comprehension. Choices define us. Under duress, in times of risk and danger, we discover what deeply matters to us: it reveals

---

1 John O'Donohue, "For a New Beginning," in *To Bless the Space Between Us* (New York: Doubleday, 2008), 14.

2 *Sophie's Choice* is a novel (later adapted to film) by William Styron about a Polish-Catholic survivor of the German Holocaust. The character, Sophie, was forced to choose which of her two children would die by gassing at a Nazi concentration camp. https://en.wikipedia.org/wiki/Sophie's_Choice_(novel)

for whom and for what purpose we will leave our zones and risk our safety and comfort. Choices lay bare for whom we feel we have "skin in the game," for whom we feel committed enough to sacrifice time and commit our resources. For whom, in extreme times, we will die. We'll revisit this topic of heart choices later.

QUESTIONS THAT MATTER

*The best and most beautiful things in the
world cannot be seen or even touched—
they must be felt with the heart.*

Helen Keller

Questions that matter—heart questions—are not meant to be answered hastily or with preconceived notions. These questions are guides and companions on our journey of self-discovery, encouraging us to enter a dialogue with our deepest selves and listen to our hearts' whispers.

These questions are inquiries that tug at our heartstrings, stirring up emotions and unearthing truths that may have remained concealed in the hustle and bustle of our lives. They can unravel layers of our experiences, revealing the roots of our self-esteem, self-worth, relationships, and sense of self. Questions, and our answers to them, form the core of our inner identities.

Questions that matter force us to confront our internalized narratives and the critical self-talk that often dominates our inner dialogue. They encourage us to challenge societal norms, explore our own stories, and rewrite scripts that no longer align with who we aspire to be.

Engaging with questions that matter is a journey into vulnerability. These questions peel back the layers of protection we've built around our hearts; they challenge us to be fully present to the triggers of our emotions. They lead us to even more profound questions that explore the depths of our being. Heart questions and answers humble us. In humility, we find the path to wholeness and authenticity.

Questions that matter empower us to bridge the gap between our inner lives and outer actions, guide us toward more purposeful and meaningful endeavors, and ultimately help us live in greater harmony with our authentic selves.

Throughout the book, you'll be offered opportunities to engage personally with the ideas presented. At times, heart questions arise as simple questions prompting us to choose wisely. Other times, the heart speaks to us through meditation or when immersed in nature.

Feel free to adapt the questions or create your own heart practice. Whatever means you choose, the purpose is cultivating a direct relationship with the heart.

Ask the questions with as much sincerity as you can muster. Write them down. Spend some time every day contemplating the questions without going into your head looking for the answers. Just be open to receiving answers from your heart.

It may take days or even weeks for some clarity to emerge. It may take patience to learn to trust that our inner wisdom will provide guidance, motivation, and courage to live our best lives.

> Many of us view questioning as a tactic to slow or defer action. When I think about the role of questions, however, I can't help but see the word "quest."
>
> *Christopher L. Kukk*

Heart Questions

1. What goals did you hold at different points in your life? Were they your goals or what others expected from you?

2. What are your dreams?

3. What fears are you not facing? When is a time you had trust in life to take risks?

Chapter 2

Tuning In to the Language of the Heart

Our normal waking consciousness, rational consciousness as we call it, is but one special type of consciousness, whilst all about it, parted from it by the filmiest of screens, there lie potential forms of consciousness entirely different.

William James

———

HEART LANGUAGE, UNLIKE the storyteller that dwells inside our head, finds expression within the senses; its knowing is intuitive and profoundly personal. Its language is unbounded—a multidimensional fusion of physical bodily sensations and emotional experiences, of "gut feelings" that defy verbal expression. It's the flutter of excitement when we see a loved one, the heaviness of grief in times of loss, and the warmth of contentment in moments of peace.

The heart often knows what the mind cannot grasp. For instance, when we're facing a significant life decision and are torn between logical reasoning and an inexplicable feeling that we're missing something important, what we're missing is hovering just beyond the horizon of our conscious awareness.

Many spiritual and meditative practices focus on tuning into sensory experiences to attain more profound awareness and understanding. Sensations can be a gateway to transcendent and heightened states of consciousness. For instance, during yoga or meditation, attuned to my body's physical sensations and tensions, I often experience quiet insights.

Moreover, our physical experiences can inform our self-perception. Someone who finds solace in running may discover that the rhythm of their breath and the sensation of their feet hitting the pavement provide moments of clarity and self-reflection. An artist may find that the tactile experience of shaping clay or the sensory richness of colors and textures evoke deep emotions that facilitate self-discovery.

Sensory experiences are thoroughly intertwined with our perceptions of the world and can elicit robust emotional responses that reveal our values and priorities. Such sensory moments become catalysts for transformation, prompting us to question our perspectives and our conditioned ideas about our place in the world.

To truly understand ourselves and others and unlock the transformative power of self-discovery, we need to listen not only to the voice of intellect but also be attuned to the richness of the world—to our bodily sensations, the emotions they arouse, and to the wisdom they provide.

THE CRUCIAL ROLE OF SENSORY EXPERIENCES

Let yourself be silently drawn by the strange pull
of what you really love. It will not lead you astray.

Rumi

Heart wisdom emerges from the interconnectedness of our emotions, sensory experiences, and intuitive understanding. This heartful way of knowing arises from the depths of our being, guiding us through life's complexities and helping us navigate the world with authenticity and compassion.

Teachers remind us that seeking wisdom in far-off places or esoteric teachings is unnecessary. Heart wisdom is innate; it reveals itself when we pause, honor, listen, and validate our inner voices, sensations, and the quiet whispers from the heart.

Sensing the heart's visceral urgings requires mindful self-awareness. It involves tuning in to our emotions, acknowledging our desires, and understanding the messages our hearts are sending us. This process can be challenging in a world that often encourages us to suppress our emotions and conform to societal expectations; where virtue-signaling instincts (wanting to look "good") encourage us to "suppress and conceal." Understanding and decoding the heart's urgings takes time, patience, and courage.

Courage is required because heart questions have the potential to elicit strong emotional responses that often touch on subjects that are deeply personal, spiritually evocative, and frequently quite challenging. We may, and likely will, come face to face with long-forgotten memories, traumas, and fears.

TUNING IN TO THE HEART'S INTUITIVE INSIGHTS

Intuitive wisdom arises when we create space below the mental chatter and embrace a receptive state of mind. When faced with a tough decision or complex challenge, allowing your awareness to penetrate your innermost core can help you connect with your deepest desires and values, often leading to choices that align more closely with your authentic self.

But what is this mysterious inner knowing? Where does it come from? And how can we trust it? Answering these questions can be transformative, taking us into subtle and elusive aspects of human consciousness.

Contrary to purely rational thought, which relies on logic and evidence, intuitive wisdom draws from a boundless well of knowledge that is beyond the reach of our conscious mind. While it may seem mystical or even mysterious, intuition is a natural and inherent part of our human experience.

Intuition, often called a "gut feeling," is a prime example of how heart wisdom is sensory wisdom. That inexplicable knowing arises within us, guiding us toward the right decisions or warning us against the wrong ones. Intuitive wisdom is revealed through sensory cues that are often too subtle to pick up on. Intuition is a way of knowing, not construed by conscious reasoning. It makes connections, sees patterns, and often arrives as a whole.

Intuition, in its purest form, is a sudden holistic awareness, an aha moment when our entire being has come together to process information from all our ways of knowing. It is a sudden completion of drawing multiple threads together in a coherent pattern. It arrives seemingly effortlessly, bringing an answer, an understanding, or recognition of how things fit together, a sense of "Oh, that's how it works!"

It takes a still body and mind to recognize this elusive energy that may arise and fade within seconds. Cultivating a still body and mind takes commitment. Some cultivate this way of knowing through meditation. It takes a certain resolve to stick to a meditative practice where progress can be as elusive as the intuitive wisdom itself—which resides at every point where the path and the destination meet without separation.

These cues are profoundly personal and arise from subjective aspects of our human experience. Different people find paths that resonate with their unique life experiences and perspectives.

It took many years before I understood my own way of knowing. I could be practical and logical in conversation, but I always lived in a bigger field. I was a teenage poet and a painter. Meditation made sense to me. Silence spoke to me. Chit-chat bored me.

I didn't understand why people wanted to discuss things they had already done. Or why anyone would like to talk about shoelaces, TV programs, or new recipes. Why would they go on in detailed narratives about events that had already happened? Most of the time, social conversations felt like wasted time, although when conversations went to things I was interested in learning, I had stamina and capacity for patience.

Although I did not understand my own process, I now know that my inner voice was filled with abstract concepts and that I was taking in feelings and experiences on a not-wordless level. I was logically well equipped, but my knowing didn't come through logical means.

Years later, I learned that my profile was INTJ in the Jungian world of personality.[3] I then found words to explain to myself what I was experiencing. I recognized that for me, knowing was not so much through sensations, or tangible physical evidence or facts, but focused on a view that sought to understand meanings and possibilities.

Knowing came to me in "gestalts," a view where I could spot connections and underlying patterns in information that it seemed others were not interested in, sometimes not

---

3 While there is controversy about the validity of the Myers-Briggs personality inventory, I find it helpful and have gained invaluable insights from the Jungian theories in which it is grounded.

immediately evident to others. I saw a constructed puzzle, how the pieces fit together, and how patterns were related to future outcomes.

The concrete, tangible world of prescribed steps for fixing, cooking, or making something held little interest, so I did my best to stay away and let my elder siblings "handle that." I sought patterns and underlying connections. Where they saw the details of a single tree, what mattered to me was the overview or under-view; the bigger picture, the view birds knew as they soared above and saw the trees' connections in the forest.

I found myself on "missions." To those near me, I could be frustratingly ignorant, sometimes hooked on things' underlying meaning and significance. I was naturally attracted to abstract ideas and possibilities.

Often I felt alone in how I saw the world. It was lonely, wanting to share but finding few companions.

I discovered a natural ability to visualize the future and plan for long-term goals, and I was willing to take risks when I believed doing so could lead to a better future outcome. I could be analytical but relied on what I now call intuition, the subconscious processing of information and patterns.

INTUITION IN MY CLINICAL WORK

As a clinician, I would often swim a mile at the end of each day. Swimming helped me decompress and finish the day by reflecting on sessions. It came without trying. I would naturally return to something that had felt dissonant, did not fit, and felt unfinished. Sometimes, I felt the emergence of a "solution," something I had not been able to see before. It was a process of holding what presented as a problem—keeping its tension close as the question hovered, its answer just out of reach.

I would crawl through the water, letting my mind wander, tracing the invisible threads of the experience that made the problem unclear until there was a click. It would come not as a linear progression of steps but as a whole picture. A sudden understanding of it came as something not calculated but as the recovery of something I knew.

The process was familiar; I had always been better at the "why" than the "how."

It wasn't gut feelings or random or educated guesses but something wordless, an abstract synthesis of information and experience that included logic but was more than logic. Like poetry. As I said, I later learned to call it intuition, a complementary way of knowing that filled in the gaps with insights not obvious or explainable in logical frameworks.

While others often appeared to rely on what they could see, hear, and touch, I accessed a sense of knowing that wasn't bound by the physical world. It was something subtle, wordless, nuanced knowledge without concrete data.

In time, I learned to trust this quiet knowing inside. I realized it would come most readily when I was quiet and when I could balance my logical knowing with my intuitive knowing.

AN EXAMPLE OF INTUITION FROM COUPLES THERAPY

The tension was palpable. Mark and Sarah[4] sat side by side, their hands clasped together, a facade of unity masking the

---

4 All client names have been changed to protect their privacy.

turmoil beneath. They had come seeking help for their struggling marriage, battered by Mark's infidelity. But as the session unfolded, a knot formed in my stomach.

Mark spoke of remorse, and a desire to rebuild trust, yet his words felt hollow. His eyes darted around the room, avoiding direct contact with Sarah. His voice, though steady, lacked conviction. He offered vague apologies and promises of change, but the underlying energy felt disingenuous.

I watched Sarah's face, her eyes filled with a desperate hope for reconciliation. She clung to his words, her need for his love blinding her to the subtle inconsistencies in his narrative. My intuition was experiencing dissonance; I felt like he was hiding something. Without evidence, only a nagging feeling, a gut instinct honed over years of working with couples, I couldn't confront him outright, risk rupturing the fragile trust we had built. Yet, I couldn't let what felt like a possible deception continue, undermining their chances for healing.

Choosing my words carefully, I turned to Mark. "I hear your words, Mark," I said, "but I sense a disconnect between what you're saying and feeling. Can you tell me more about what's happening inside you right now?"

He hesitated, his facade momentarily faltering. A flicker of panic crossed his face before he regained his composure. He offered a well-rehearsed response, reiterating his commitment to change. But the seed of doubt had been planted.

In the following sessions, I gently probed, creating a safe space for Sarah to express her doubts and fears. I encouraged Mark to explore his inner conflict and confront the truth he was hiding from himself and his wife. It was a slow, painstaking process, but eventually, the cracks in his facade widened, and the truth emerged.

On the day the truth came out, Mark told Sarah the affair had continued, the shame and guilt pouring out of him. It was a devastating blow for Sarah but also a turning point. With the truth out in the open, they could begin deciding whether they wanted to try to rebuild their relationship.

My intuition hadn't been proof, but it had been a guiding light. An attunement to an unspoken truth beneath the surface of words and actions.

MORE THREADS OF MY KNOWING

It was 1974. I was once more in the middle of what may have been a clinical depression. Walking around one of the lakes of Minneapolis one evening, I saw a charming home a little bit off the shore of the lake across the road. I stopped to look closer and saw a sign listing the Minnesota Zen Meditation Center meditation hour. I saw that I could walk into the beginning of the meditation teaching session. I walked in. Norm Randolph was teaching. For the first time, I sat on a round black pillow. It felt as if I had come home. I had no idea yet what I had tasted that unplanned quiet evening. But it was the first taste of the stillness that is still my refuge place today. I learned how to rest there, and I came to think of it as the quiet ocean of my heart.

Many years later, when I learned to scuba dive in the actual ocean, I allowed myself to freefall in the water's depths and hover, feeling my body rise and fall with my breath—neutrally buoyant, just totally still, the sparkling of fish hovering silently around me in what I regarded as the primordial womb of life, the sea.

The quiet ocean of our heart is the place of intuition, as well as inspiration. It's where we can find direction, inspiration, and courage to act wisely, if we're paying attention.

WHEN URGENCY AND INSPIRATION MEET

In the quiet stillness of my office, a young woman named Ann sat across from me, her eyes clouded with a mix of guilt and regret. She recounted an incident with her beloved daughter, where in a moment of panic, she reacted harshly to prevent her youngster from potential harm. Ann's voice wavered as she described the sharp words that had escaped her lips, the fear that had flickered in her daughter's eyes. Regret hung heavy in the air. It was not a single occasion but a pattern.

Months later, Ann brought a new story, a subtle shift in her demeanor. She shared a similar scenario with her daughter, yet a different story unfolded this time. Instead of reacting impulsively, she had paused, recognizing the opportunity for gentle guidance. Her concern for her child's safety remained, but it no longer fueled a knee-jerk reaction.

Ann had redirected her daughter with a newfound sense of calm, her words laced with love and understanding. It wasn't without its challenges; echoes of her past behavior had tempted her to act out. But she had persevered in self-regulation, choosing compassion over fear, connection over control. She could transcend the temptation to act it out. Her heart had counseled restraint this time.

As Ann finished her story, a smile had bloomed on her face, a radiant expression of self-discovery. She spoke of taming her impulsive responses, of cultivating a space for mindful action even amidst worry and concern.

Ann's journey mirrored the path of countless others: a dance between fear and love, reactivity and responsiveness. In the face of our own imperfections, we can learn to regulate, to pause. We can choose to meet life's challenges with an open heart, transforming not only our relationships with others but also our relationships with ourselves.

My own recollection about urgency comes with humility. It happened on a Wednesday evening, at 6:20. I was scheduled to begin on Zoom at 6:30. I had led a guided meditation group online for years. And the meeting wasn't working; I couldn't get in. I panicked. I am tech-challenged and always approach tech-related responsibilities with a feeling of dread.

With ten minutes left, I called my neighbor (an Apple employee) for help, and with five minutes to spare, she arrived. I was frozen with fear, but she was cheerful, light-hearted, and upbeat and casually sat down at my desk to see what she could do to help.

As I stood beside her, the clocks relentlessly ticking loud in my mind, she started to tell a story about her two-year-old. I snapped. My voice filled with irritation and impatience; I reminded her I had only minutes before I went "on." She froze, turned to the keyboard, did what she needed to do, and left without a word.

In my practice, I have often noted how the word *over-whelm* has the word *helm* in it. Like a temporarily disabled captain of a ship, I had allowed my sense of urgency to over-ride my wise judgment and better knowing. I had allowed my fear that I could not show up to hijack me and lead me to make a choice I regretted.

As I sat down, I could feel the chemicals in my body begin to subside. I was filled with remorse. Such an irony! I was leading meditation but not walking the talk! I groaned to myself as I felt the adrenaline rush subside, and I knew I would apologize.

Yet I can think of other times when urgency has had a different impact and filled me with a sense of mission and purpose. A *force* of commitment. I felt it when I walked in marches—disciplined, determined, committed to nonvio-lence but unrelenting in purpose, singing the Pete Seeger song "We Shall Not Be Moved." I remember how I walked together with a shared determination to not allow racism to continue, to pursue change unwaveringly, and to continue to march for change until we succeeded.

Like a drumbeat compelling us forward, urgency, with its relentless pulse, compels us to move, make decisions swiftly, and confront challenges head-on. It's a call to action, the catalyst that pushes us beyond our comfort zones.

However, urgency alone can lead to a frantic rush, driven by fear or time pressure, blurring our focus and clouding our judgment. When driven solely by urgency, we may find ourselves in a perpetual cycle of reactive responses, navigating a sea of tasks without a clear sense of direction. If not tempered, the frenetic energy of urgency might eclipse the quiet whispers from our hearts.

On the other hand, inspiration sparks a fire that propels us forward, not through fear or anxiety, but with a sense of purpose and passion. It's a gentle yet potent force that whispers truths to our hearts, illuminating our path and infusing our actions with meaning and significance.

The beauty of inspiration is its ability to transform urgency into meaningful action. When we fuse urgency with inspiration, we cultivate a harmonious balance. Urgency becomes the fuel that propels us forward, while inspiration serves as our North Star, guiding us toward our true intentions. In this union, we find a rhythm—a cadence that allows us to move swiftly yet deliberately, with a clear understanding of our purpose.

Where urgency and inspiration meet, we're propelled by clarity and conviction. It's where bold ideas that transcend the moment's immediacy take root. It's where we learn to respond with intention rather than react to the moment's demands.

In Dutch, *dringend* describes something that *is* urgent, while *urgentie* refers to the *concept* or *level* of urgency itself.

Embracing the convergence of urgency and inspiration requires a mindful awareness—acknowledging the urgency without succumbing to its frantic pace and cultivating inspiration without drifting into mere daydreaming. It calls for a deliberate pause—a moment to listen to the whispers of inspiration amid the cacophony of urgency.

WHEN THE HEART OPENS

A disciple asks the rebbe: "Why does Torah tell us to
'place these words upon your hearts?' Why does it not
tell us to place these holy words in our hearts?"
The rebbe answers: "It is because as we are,
our hearts are closed, and we cannot place the
holy words in our hearts. So, we place them on
top of our hearts. And there they stay until one
day, the heart breaks, and the words fall in."

Ancient Hasidic tale

When the heart closes, we cut ourselves off from our own power. We become afraid to take risks, to express our true selves, and to connect with others on a deep level. We feel lonely, isolated, judgmental, and often cynical as our world becomes smaller and smaller—the size of a boat without a rudder.

But an open heart has a way of cutting through the noise and helping us discern what truly matters. When attuned to matters of the heart, we're more likely to make decisions that align with our authentic selves and live meaningful lives of purpose and significance.

We break free from rigid belief systems and prejudices when the heart opens. We're better able to embrace our inherent vulnerability rather than fear, to shed at last our protective shell and allow our true selves, warts and all, to be seen by others. We become relatable, approachable, and reliable. We become authentically who we are.

When the heart opens, the walls of the ego soften, and our reach and embrace expand. The heart becomes a vessel for empathy, allowing us to step into the shoes of others and experience their joys and sorrows, and giving us the ability to offer genuine support. This empathetic connection transcends boundaries, leading to a broader perspective that is inclusive and accepting of diverse cultures, beliefs, and experiences. Our life is enriched by this connection and empowered by a sense of responsibility.

When one heart opens, brimming with empathy and compassion, it lays the foundation for a more just, harmonious, and inclusive society. Social and environmental issues are approached with a sense of urgency and responsibility, with the realization that the well-being of one is the well-being of all.

As hearts around the world open, a global paradigm shift has the potential to catalyze collaborative efforts toward ending world hunger, inequality, and environmental degradation.

Courageous men never lose the zest for living
even though their life situation is zestless; cowardly
men, overwhelmed by the uncertainties of life,
lose the will to live. We must constantly build
dikes of courage to hold back the flood of fear.

Martin Luther King, Jr., from Strength to Love

Heart Questions

1. Recall a time when you were compelled by fear and a driving sense of urgency that led to undesired consequences.

2. What was the driving feeling behind this overpowering sense of urgency?

3. Imagine (and rewrite) how it could have been different if you'd waited for clarity and inspiration to emerge.

Chapter 3

Recognizing Potholes on the Heart's Journey

Revere those things beyond science which really
matter and about which it is so difficult to speak.

Werner Heisenberg

———

NOW THAT WE'VE tuned into the sensory language of our
heart and gut, let's get to know some of the potholes created by our brain's proclivity to get stuck or lost in fearful
scenarios, to freeze in the complexity around us, and to be
distracted by the noise of today's world.

Without a doubt, the human brain is a marvel of evolution,
brimming with extraordinary potential. It has steered the
course of civilizations, birthed technologies that reshaped
our lives, and held keys to our mysterious universe.

The heart knows something else: it recognizes the difference between knowledge and wisdom, between information
and meaning. Whereas the brain asks questions requiring
logic, reason, and often depends on calculators, telescopes,
and particle colliders, the heart asks questions requiring us
to navigate the inner terrain of emotions, vulnerabilities, and
convictions. While both ways of knowing are essential, our
brains prefer questions that clarify and bring closure rather
than those that confound.

Heart questions, on the other hand, often confound. They
often take us out of our comfort zone. Heart questions arise

when we experience events and feelings that challenge what we think we know, even what we have accepted is "right" and "true." Our inner struggles with fear, ambiguity, paradox, ambivalence, and our deepest beliefs about ourselves and the world we live in all arise in the realm of the heart.

While intellectual knowledge offers a sense that "I am right," the heart lives with doubt and uncertainty, with ambiguity, which can throw us off our game and shake the very ground we stand on. Confronted with this discomfort, we may dig in our heels and cling to what we think we know. We may also find courage that allows us to dare to trust and employ our critical thinking, and to open to the possibility of new ways of seeing and knowing. But finding our bravery means facing our fears.

NAVIGATING FEAR IN THE TERRAIN OF THE HEART

For most of us, fear is a lifelong companion, often arising as a valid, protective response. Our innate fear responses arises not only at times of physical danger. In his book *The Denial of Death*, Ernest Becker argues that we are as much afraid of dying without meaning as we fear physical extinction. Fear is also triggered by what we experience as threats to our ego. We shudder at the possibility of rejection, criticism, failure, and evidence of incompetence or cowardice. Fear of exposure propels us to find ways to "airbrush" and embellish, to minimize the risk of exposing parts of us we don't want to face, parts we don't want to know, and parts we don't want others to see. We create barriers to escape and avoid those difficult aspects of who we are and the challenges they bring.

Barriers can take the form of addictions as well as inner defenses such as denial, repression, avoidance, and projection.

Over time, defenses create layers of opaqueness that shroud awareness. We become like a house, where one part is kept in open view, while the other (the stuff that confuses as well as what we want to hide and keep from dealing with) is carefully guarded, locked behind a door to the basement. That closed door can keep us unconsciously or willfully ignorant but imprisoned.

To free ourselves from ideals of perfection and live in self-acceptance of our authentic selves, we need to dismantle those barriers and bring our "shadow" (the unwanted, denied, or unclaimed aspects of ourselves) into open view. That means looking inward, opening the closed doors, and welcoming those "split off" parts with compassion and understanding. In the journey to integrated wholeness and self-awareness, we can learn to "tame" those shadow parts of ourselves.

One of my clients who had spent years on this journey described it: "It's a paradox! I feel perfectly imperfect now. I feel more in charge of myself, treat myself as I do my kids, accept them as they are, and set limits and boundaries. I'm more in charge of my own 'I, me, my, mine' tendencies!"

> But fear of making mistakes can itself become a
> huge mistake, one that prevents you from living,
> for life is risky and anything less is already loss.
>
> *Rebecca Solnit*

ENDURING FEAR, UNCERTAINTY, AND DOUBT

We all grapple with fear, uncertainty, and doubt. At some point, we all fear making the wrong choice, being judged by others, suffering humiliation, or losing something important to us. Fear ignites uncertainty; we hesitate to take risks in pursuing our passions. Worse, fear can cause us to doubt our ability to stay the course.

When fear captures us, we retreat into these self-made cages, reluctant to open our hearts. We feel constrained and guarded, afraid to be vulnerable. The fear of rejection or betrayal leaves us with even more stagnation and isolation. We feel trapped. Robbed of meaningful connections. Robbed of a full life. And unable or unwilling to recognize that we're doing it to ourselves.

Fear feeds self-limiting beliefs, convincing us we're not worthy of love, happiness, or success. These beliefs can become deeply ingrained and difficult to overcome, hindering personal growth and our commitment to a heart-oriented life.

The relentless nature of fear, uncertainty, and doubt can be a formidable obstacle. The head may stop us, but the heart knows we can confront our fears, we can do hard things, and we can take just one more forward step.

And then another.

FACING THE DISCOMFORT OF CONFLICTING BELIEFS

I once had a counseling client named Alia, a bright-eyed girl who had migrated with her family to Minneapolis. She went to public school, excelling in her studies, and was learning to adapt to her new life. Yet a subtle dissonance gnawed at her. At home, Alia had learned to be compliant, to defer to the voices of her father and brothers. She was loyal to cultural norms, knowing her behavior was linked to family honor. But she faced cultural challenges in school, where teachers encouraged her to speak her mind openly and freely with her male as well as female classmates. The change had started to feel familiar, even natural, but it tested her family- and faith-conditioned beliefs.

This difference created a constant internal struggle. Alia felt torn between the cultural and religious gender rules of her family and the newfound freedoms of her adopted home. She longed to express herself "in the American way," but the fear of disrespecting traditional patterns and religious ordinances made it "feel wrong."

One day, during a class discussion, Alia passionately disagreed with a point made by a male classmate. She was confident in her own truth, and the words were ready. Feeling the inner dissonance, she hesitated for a moment and then decided. Alia took a deep breath.

"I see it differently," she began, as she stood up from her classroom desk, shaking slightly. It was a small step, but speaking her truth that day marked the beginning of Alia's journey to reconcile the two worlds she lived in as an immigrant.

I listened and felt compassion for the young girl. I knew the choices she was confronting. I knew the cost. I too had lived through what she was experiencing.

We all strive for consistency and harmony within our thoughts, beliefs, and values. When inconsistencies or contradictions arise, we experience a sense of unease. We may become irritable, agitated, and confused. We may feel a loss of control and feelings of powerlessness. This conflicted internal state is called cognitive dissonance, and it's more common than you may think.

Sometimes this dissonance arises when our hearts open to deeper reflection. Sometimes it comes when we encounter new information and insights that challenge existing beliefs and self-perceptions. Sometimes it comes when aspects of ourselves that we're not proud of emerge, forcing us to reconsider long-held beliefs. At these times, we may draw new conclusions, make new decisions, and then question those choices. Doubts about our ability to discern follow. We find ourselves struggling with regret. We feel unclear and anxious.

The rippling effects of cognitive dissonance can be wide-ranging. Our relationships and interactions with others may be affected. External influences—such as societal expectations, family dynamics, or cultural norms—can become yet another source of anxiety, making it even harder to access our feelings or articulate our thoughts.

While enduring the discomfort of cognitive dissonance can lead to valuable insights about yourself and your relationships, it can also lead to resistance, defensiveness, or avoidance, especially if the conflicting beliefs are deeply ingrained or challenging to confront. Doubting our ability to successfully navigate these thresholds of transformation can be a significant hurdle.

MY OWN COGNITIVE DISSONANCE WITH FAITH

The church of my childhood was a place where unwavering faith was taught and practiced daily. My family read the Children's Bible together after every meal, and the teachings of Jesus were etched into my heart. Yet, as I grew older, a stark contrast emerged between the ideals professed by the church and the reality of its actions.

This dissonance became painfully clear when I was a teenager in a local Canadian school and assigned to read Alan Paton's book *Cry, the Beloved Country*. I learned that the leaders of the Dutch Reformed Church, my church, supported the pro-apartheid regime. It seemed to me that the church was oppressing Black Christians in South Africa with their own Christian religion. I heard the words, the reasoning, used to defend the regime, but my heart listened to the cry Paton had written about.

The church's acceptance of apartheid in South Africa created dissonance within me. How could a community claiming to follow the teachings of love and equality support a system rooted in segregation and injustice? My youthful idealism and how I understood the life of Jesus clashed with the church's action in the world. The dissonance gnawed at my soul. When I voiced my concerns, I was met with defensiveness and dismissal, and a Bible-based story that supposedly justified apartheid. I couldn't "buy it." It led to profound distrust and a shaken faith.

The crux of my disillusionment was not the expectation that the church or Christians be perfect. I understood and accepted that we are fallible. What I could not accept was the lack of acknowledgment and accountability for what I saw as glaring inconsistencies. I experienced it as hypocrisy: the words and deeds did not match what I had learned from the life and teachings of Jesus. These contradictions created confusion and betrayal; I began to doubt. As a teen, I started to go my way quietly: I "secretly" participated in activities like dancing and going to the movies—these too, once condemned as sinful, were yet later embraced without explanation. The inconsistencies between what was said to be morally wrong and ordained by the Bible and later accepted (without explanation or accountability) made me question if some so-called "moral" issues were cultural or personal subjective preferences rather than true morality.

The church's refusal to own its mistakes and its defensive responses eroded its credibility. For me, it wasn't just about being wrong about some things; I could understand how views change over time. What made me back away was not "sin" but the unwillingness to admit to "sin." This lack of accountability made me question the sincerity of the faith I had been raised with. I began to see how religion could be used as a tool of power and control, especially among immigrant communities—besieged with change and challenges to adapt—where church beliefs were sometimes (to me, conveniently) wielded to enforce conformity.

Despite the disillusionment, I held onto the teachings of Jesus, which seemed pure and true. However, the dogmatic interpretation that governed the church's actions often conflicted with the values it claimed to uphold. It pushed me to critically examine the beliefs I had been raised with, ultimately reshaping my understanding of morality and spirituality.

My cognitive dissonance created an opportunity for reflection and growth. Still, I spent painful years living in a "no man's land," a bare desert of existential doubt and sometimes despair. I came to rest when my heart and mind found a path that aligned with my critically examined beliefs.

THE MASKS OF CONFORMITY

We live in a culture that rewards conformity and linear thinking. We don masks that conceal our authentic selves, fearing the unveiling of our innermost desires and vulnerabilities. The desire to belong, to be accepted, can shroud us in a veneer that obscures our true essence.

We craft our identities as if sculpting a masterpiece, shaping our thoughts, words, and actions to mirror those around us. Fearing rejection or isolation if our true colors were to shine through, we paint our masks with the hues of societal approval. Beneath this carefully constructed façade, our inner landscape remains obscured, our individuality suppressed. Parts of us remain imprisoned, yearning for delivery.

But if we dare, if we choose, we may peel back the layers of this mask of conformity, our need for approval, and venture into the wild, uncharted territory of authenticity.

RESISTING A LIFE OF CONFORMITY

Alex came to my office in the first year of my practice. Today, more than 40 years later, I still remember him. In truth, I was a little daunted when I discovered that he came from vast wealth; his background very different from mine.

In many ways, he was like others his age. He wore the same clothes but had grown up in the unspoken norms of Bronxville and had recently moved to the Midwest.

He came to therapy to talk about a decision he was making. He said, "I know you may think I'm crazy, but I've only got one life. I just need to run it by someone unbiased."

Alex had been groomed for success and born into a lineage of inherited wealth, generations of real estate barons and lawyers. He talked about breaking the ties of a family legacy of wealth-generating professions.

While "at home," he had easily navigated the Ivy League, eventually attaining a PhD in Chinese history. He loved that history but yearned for a different path. "I want to live with soil in my hands, to live with the rhythm of the seasons; I want to grow food." I quietly breathed in and held my tongue as I started considering what this would mean for him as the firstborn, the only son in his family.

As I listened quietly, Alex went on, describing how he had visited his beloved grandfather, who had retired early to live on a farm in Wisconsin. Alex had stayed for the summer and sensed the older man's peace, his connection to the land, and his deep respect for the natural world. "It was so radically different from anything I had experienced. I fell in love with the land," he said, looking at me, a deep, severe conviction in the direct gaze of his sky-blue eyes.

I sensed that he had felt a calling.

I had only a few sessions with Alex after that first visit, but several years later, he was in town and came to tell me how his life turned out.

Alex's unwavering resolve had shocked his family and peers, who met the news of his move to a farm with disbelief, even anger. His parents pleaded with him to reconsider, but with a determination that invoked their eventual respect, he risked losing their approval, even their love, to live a life true to himself.

"Maybe in your words, Doc," he said, "'I could do no other,' and I'm glad for it."

Years before the organic food movement gained momentum, Alex became a pioneer, a visionary ahead of his time. Supported by his love of the land and his unwavering belief, he became a leader in sustainable agriculture.

In time, Alex's family came to accept his path. They witnessed the joy he found in his work and the fulfillment he derived from nurturing the land. They saw the positive impact he had on his community and the environment. And in their way, they came to respect his choices, even to admire his courage.

Daring to defy expectations and challenge family and cultural norms, Alex carved his path, found personal fulfillment, and contributed to a movement that would change how we think about food and our relationship to the natural world.

THE NOISE OF DISTRACTION
AND THE FEAR OF SILENCE

Our media, our culture of ceaseless activity, and our constant pursuit of achievement make it easy to get swept away by a torrent of thoughts, demands, and expectations. With so much mental noise, we can quickly feel disconnected from the actual world and eventually, ourselves.

The noise of distraction constantly draws us away from the heart's richness and stillness, leaving in its wake an odd sort of discomfort in our own company. Persistent mental chatter can drive us to fill every moment with busyness, like an insidious pothole that arises from an unlikely source: a deep-rooted fear of silence.

Have you ever tried to find a way to escape from someone who pounces to fill each empty moment with verbal noise? Have you had the experience of being with someone who pauses, not to listen but for the cue that you are done so they can leap in with their following comment? Have you ever feared what might arise during moments of introspection, that silence within?

The fear of silence can propel us and perpetuate a cycle of surface-level engagement. We hold conversations where we skim the surface of things, communicating with little real listening. Without the capacity or willingness to pause, to be still and listen to each other's hearts, we fail to delve into the depths of understanding. When we do not engage, we fail to meet each other with intentional care and empathy.

At such times, we may sense something missing, and we are left hungry for something more: the engagement in openhearted presence, the caring listening, and reciprocity that nurtures genuine connections with others, the world, and ourselves.

Parker J. Palmer offers recurring threads of wisdom in his writings that encourage us to willingly embrace solitude and silence, allow ourselves the space to reflect, listen to our heart's murmurs, and connect with our innermost selves. But we don't have to do it alone. In his book *A Hidden Wholeness*, he writes:

> It takes good friends to sustain silence and laughter because both make us vulnerable. Silence makes us vulnerable because when we stop making noise, we lose control: who knows what thoughts or feelings might arise if we turned off the television or stopped yammering for a while? Laughter makes us vulnerable because it often comes in response to our flaws and foibles: who knows how foolish we might look when the joke is on us? We can share silence and laughter only when we trust each other—and the more often we share them, the deeper our trust grows.[5]

SHADOWS FROM THE PAST

Of course, we must discern when and with whom we can trust to share our darkest feelings. Not everything is safe;

---

5   Parker J. Palmer. *A Hidden Wholeness: The Journey Toward an Undivided Life* (San Francisco, CA: Jossey-Bass, 2004), 152.

not everyone can be trusted to hold another's heart with care. We all have had experiences in our lives that branded us emotionally. As children, most of our attention is on our inner world, on how we feel. Children do not have the analytical facilities to process a cruel or painful event, to understand fully what happened in order to accurately attribute the cause and explain why it occurred. When a child is told that something "bad" or "wrong" happened, they may automatically assume they are the source and blame themselves.

Speaking from my clinical experience, I've seen that it is almost impossible for a child to take in that a parent or family member is selfishly meeting their own needs at the child's expense. That reality can be unbearable, can make their world entirely unsafe. It is better to think "it's me," and that "I am provoking and to blame, as I am being told." For the child, this view provides the possibility for change and hope, as they reason, "I can't change my parent, but perhaps if I am the cause, *I can then change* and prevent this from happening again." The child begins to accept the self as the cause and begins to regulate.

As adults, however, when some painful event happens, we are more inclined to look *outside* ourselves to find the cause. Then, once we identify a cause, we seek to separate ourselves from it. If pain happened at a dentist appointment, we begin to fear dentists. If it happened in a storm, we may forever avoid storms. If the experience involved someone who spoke and looked a certain way, we may avoid that person or people with similar characteristics. Or, say it involved a dog; we forever hate all dogs. You probably know someone who has had such an experience.

We tend to carry our prejudices and biases into our relationships, marriages, and careers. Every experience is measured against something that happened to us in the past. Over and over, we use the present to confirm the past. When we live in the shadow of some painful experience, our past becomes our future.

MILAREPA'S CAVE

A Tibetan friend once told me the story of "Milarepa's Cave," which is also recounted by the renowned American Buddhist nun Pema Chödrön in her book *Start Where You Are*.[6] It's an ancient Tibetan parable about surrendering to, rather than avoiding, the common but complex "potholes" in the terrain of the heart.

> One evening, Milarepa returned to his cave after gathering firewood, only to find it filled with demons. They were cooking his food, reading his books, sleeping in his bed. They'd taken over the joint . . . . Even though he had the sense that they were just a projection of his own mind—all the unwanted parts of himself—he didn't know how to get rid of them.
>
> So first he taught them the dharma. He sat on this seat that was higher than they were and said things to them about how we are all one. He talked about compassion and shunyata and how poison is medicine. Nothing happened. The demons were still there. Then he lost his patience and got angry and ran at them. They just laughed at him. Finally, he gave up and just sat down

---

6 Pema Chödrön. *Start Where You Are: A Guide to Compassionate Living*, (Boulder: Shambhala, 2018) 35–36.

on the floor, saying, "I'm not going away and it looks like you're not either, so let's just live here together."

At that point, all of them left except one. Milarepa said, "Oh, this one is particularly vicious.". . . He didn't know what to do, so he surrendered himself even further. He walked over and put himself right into the mouth of the demon and said, "Just eat me up if you want to." Then that demon left too.

When we wholeheartedly accept the complexities of a life lived through the heart, our mind can befriend those events and enter a portal to something extraordinary. When we're forced to turn to others and accept help, we learn interdependency. When we've exhausted every avenue, we turn inward. Day by day, we become stronger, more resilient, more authentically who we are, who we've always been—and now, can finally meet.

> Facing the darkness, admitting the pain,
> allowing the pain to be pain, is never easy.
> This is why courage–big-heartedness–is the
> most essential virtue on the spiritual journey.
>
> *Matthew Fox*

Heart Questions

1. Of the "potholes" discussed in this chapter—fear, uncertainty, doubt, conformity, fear of silence—which one comes up most frequently for you? How do you react?

2. When have you experienced a divergence between what you thought you should do and what you wanted to do?

3. What would it look like to surrender, like Milarepa, to one of your heart's unwanted "demons?"

PART II

Reclaiming the Heart, Again and Again

Behold the One in all things;
it is the second that leads you astray.

Kabir

Chapter 4

To Lose Heart
Is to Lose Yourself

Whether all is really lost or not depends
entirely on whether or not I am lost.

Václav Havel

—————

MY FATHER WAS 48 when I was born. We lived in Holland, in a town called Giessendam, on the river Beneden-Merwede. A stream from that river flowed as close to our home as my garage sits near my home today. A high *dijk* was the main road, and young willows grew on the river's edge, their soft bark sometimes stripped to make *hoepels*, bands that would be used to gird barrels and casks. The year was 1941, I was the eighth of eight children, and our little village had been under German occupation for the past year.

Armed Nazis policed our streets, raided our homes, darkened our skies with bombers, imposed curfews and restrictions. Everyone had to register with the Germans. Able-bodied men between the ages of 16 and 45 disappeared, conscripted into Nazi labor camps.

I am told that when I was a baby and the bombing was heavy, I would sleep in my father's bed; he was ever careful not to roll on me in his sleep. A tin washtub with two handles would be ready on the floor so I could be quickly moved to the tub and carried to the bomb shelter when air raid sirens told us to flee.

As a toddler, I was a happy and energetic little thing, I'm told, and very close to my father, following him around, tugging at his hair and ears. I knew I was his *klein beesje*, a Dutch endearment that means "sweet little animal," like a playful kitten—always spoken with tenderness and a glint in his eye. He was always gentle with me and patient, much like a grandfather, which may seem normal for a man his age. However, these were not normal times, and my father's steadfast forbearance was far beyond average.

I'm told that when I came along, I was a much-needed diversion from the bone-deep fear that permeated our small village, often turning neighbor against neighbor, as some sought favor and extra food rations from the Nazis in exchange for information—information that could mean imprisonment, conscription, or death for a neighbor.

Before the German invasion and occupation of Holland, we were an upper-middle-class family, influential and respected in our small town, which consisted of only a few roads and dikes and a few thousand people. My elder siblings were students, unaware that soon their education would end, as the occupiers used school buildings for their headquarters. When the Nazis invaded overnight, everything changed on a dime. The change would last more than five years.

From my perspective, my father never lost heart throughout the war. Nor afterward when circumstances made him decide to take our family to Canada. The post-war economic recovery plan restricted emigrating people from taking currency out of the Netherlands, and thus, we came penniless. It was a ten-day voyage across the Atlantic to Canada in a converted army troop carrier, then three days by train from Quebec to Toronto, where our sponsor met us and brought us to our new home. That first week, I turned eight.

As it turned out, we would live in a shared farmhouse four miles from Schomberg, a small town in Ontario that today, 75-plus years later, is sometimes used for movie settings because of its quaintness. My mother's first impression was dismay. I remember how she cried out in horror, "It's a chicken coop! We are to live in a chicken coop?" The pump where we drew and carried all our water in buckets (my dad said his arms lengthened because of the weight) was a good 150 yards away from the house, in a pigsty.

When our two wooden boxes of belongings eventually arrived, one box became the outhouse. The contaminated well water became the reason for our next move. When my mother was later hospitalized for cancer surgery, she received a colostomy that needed to be irrigated as part of her daily care, but the water at home was unclean. For a while, water was brought in by car daily by someone who lived in Schomberg. It was expensive. Eventually, we left and moved to Hamilton, a big city.

Like me, my father was an introvert. A quiet man with a sharp and curious mind, despite only a fourth-grade education, he'd devised algebraic solutions for his business ventures. I knew he was intelligent and sharp. But I also knew he carried the weight of bringing his family to a new world with nothing but hope and determination. He didn't speak of it, but I could sense his grief. Dad never complained and somehow managed to carry us through and keep us safe. He never showed a loss of courage or fortitude. His intellectual curiosity, his sense of humor, and conviction prevailed through it all.

As I said, my mother was diagnosed with cancer and required a colostomy almost immediately after immigrating. My sister Betsy, who had experienced five years of war followed by dislocation in her 17-year-young life, manifested symptoms of what I now, as a clinical psychologist, believe was PTSD. For more than two years, she was institutional-ized in an Ontario provincial mental hospital where she was administered insulin shock and electrical shock treatment. After those years of involuntary confinement, Betsy died years later after surgery that removed a brain tumor. Both cancer and mental illness were considered sources of shame in the 1950s, commonly hidden from public knowledge. My mother succumbed to that shame and, from that time on, was a recluse, not leaving her home and garden (where she grew roses and peonies) for anything but medical appointments.

We had no health insurance, and the medical bills were twice the mortgage payments on our first and only house. Everyone worked to pay off that debt. Once a village leader and member of the Resistance, my father became a day laborer, first for a Canadian contractor. We all anglicized our names, and in time, my father and my brothers established the Demik Construction Company.

How did he *not* completely lose heart? Once I caught a glimpse.

Even as a child, I was drawn to art, particularly the work of van Gogh. His paintings were familiar—not surpris-ing, since he'd created some just a few kilometers from my home, capturing landscapes much like mine. One painting of a man bent forward, head in his hands, moved me deeply. His eyes were hidden, but I imagined him consumed by fear and despair.

One day, in the quiet barn far from our farmhouse in Shomberg, I saw van Gogh's painting mirrored in my father. The barn was still, a shard of sunlight illuminating his shoul-der, which then moved, and I realized he was weeping. He was dressed much like van Gogh's man, bowed over in the same way, head on his hand. My father must have found a private space to grieve, and I backed away, not wanting him to know I had witnessed his vulnerability. But the image stayed with me. I thought of him as in the Bible, where Jesus was prophesied as "a man of sorrow and acquainted with grief." I knew he had forever left his 12 brothers and sisters, his parents. News of their deaths came from letters. There was no money for travel back to his home country.

To this day, whenever I lose my heart, I call on his memory to remember how he lived during those most perilous times. In the depths of my being, I feel grateful and bolstered. As my heart reopens, I begin to "come to myself" again.

> He who works with his hands is a laborer.
> He who works with his hands and his head
> is a craftsman. He who works with his hands
> and his head and his heart is an artist.
>
> *St. Francis of Assisi*

RECLAIMING LOST GROUND

When the heart loses its ground, it has to be reclaimed. Perhaps this metaphor comes from my subconscious, from deep-seated roots in my homeland of the Netherlands, which literally means "lower countries." A quarter of Holland's land is below sea level in areas known as *polders*, the result of land reclamation that began in the 14th century.

I've often read that the Dutch reclaimed their land from the sea, but in fact, they claimed and reclaimed it over and over again. The land of Holland belonged as much to the North Sea as it did to the continent. Geologically, land is constantly shifting. High tides, flooding, and wind cause erosion. There's a saying, "God created the world, but the Dutch created the Netherlands." For more than 700 years, the Dutch have built dikes to hold back the water and create the polders that are used for farming. The windmills familiar in my earliest years and commonly associated with quintessential Dutch land-scapes were used to pump water out because rivers keep flowing, rains keep raining, and tides keep rising.

Once the Dutch claimed the land, they constantly nur-tured, cultivated, and reclaimed it. The land is vulnerable just as the heart is vulnerable.

My father told me that whenever there is the possibility of a dike breach from high waves or heavy rains (I think this is still true in Holland), everyone in the village is on an early warning system called "dike watch." Each villager knows exactly what to do, where the sandbags are stored, and how to place them to prevent ruin.

For me, "dike watch" has become a metaphor. The heart, too, needs an early warning system, an ever-present reminder of its vulnerability to erosion and invasion.

The demands of today's world—no matter where we live—require that we stay vigilant in cultivating, claiming, and reclaiming our hearts. We are all subject to inner and outer influences, not least the intrinsically existing "sins of the heart" I learned about as a kid: envy, gluttony, greed, lust, pride, sloth, and wrath. We are inundated by invasions of the mind or invasions of the culture that wash over us (like the cultural shifts that can flood us with hatred, polarization, and isolation).

That's why we must cultivate awareness and readiness for resistance, positive *inner resistance*. Resistance isn't just against Nazis.

When the heart loses its ground, it *must* be reclaimed.

INDIVIDUALISM OR INTERCONNECTION?

We are living in an age obsessed with individual achievement, a relentless pursuit of autonomy fueled by a capitalist engine that demands constant growth, a pursuit inextricably linked to exploiting our planet's resources. We're consuming the earth to achieve our so-called "good life."

These days I sometimes feel overwhelmed. I blame it on age or technology, but I don't think it is only my generational slowness that cripples me. Tech promises to liberate me, to give me more time. But the reality is quite different. We're trapped in a cycle of perpetual busyness—constantly upgrading, complying, and reacting to the endless stream of notifications and demands. We've become slaves to the very technology that was supposed to set us free. The result? Less time for the things that truly matter, the things that nurture our hearts, our relationships, and our souls.

We're chasing "more"—more resources, more freedom, more *stuff*—but in doing so, we're losing something essential. We're neglecting our inner lives, sacrificing meaning for material accumulation. It's a kind of spiritual erosion. We're becoming experts in the external world but strangers to our inner landscapes. This relentless pursuit of more is a pursuit of madness. I may be an old prophet, but it seems that this path leads not to fulfillment but to a profound sense of emptiness and disconnection.

I am a personal champion of independence and individualism. Myself an immigrant, I can see how these qualities allowed early settlers, rebels, and explorers to survive; that possessing these qualities of independence may have made them uniquely suited to endure and navigate the dangers and complex challenges of pioneer life.

But the ideals of individualism and reverence for independence remain today so embedded in our culture that we barely notice the individualistic demands that inform our decisions and thinking. Most of us grew up with movies of the American hero, often represented as being unfettered by restraints, going alone, needing no one, having no lasting relationships, and living outside society.

It makes one wonder. It may be that early settlers were self-selectively more individually resilient by nature or necessity. It could also be that these were myths of Hollywood that for dramatic reasons left out the simple reality that even these early "characters" required companions and community.

Rugged individualism emphasizes self-reliance, personal freedom, and individual achievement and embodies the spirit of self-sufficiency and personal autonomy. It celebrates the idea that individuals should be free to pursue their goals, make independent decisions, and reap the rewards of their hard work. It's at the core of capitalism. Its proponents argue that it fosters innovation, entrepreneurship, and personal growth. It encourages individuals to take risks, challenge conventions, and contribute to society through unique skills and talents.

There is no doubt that individualism can empower people to overcome adversity, cultivate resilience, and embrace their identities. It allows for the exploration of diverse perspectives and the protection of individual rights and liberties. Rugged individualism can manifest as a sense of personal responsibility as individuals take ownership of their choices and outcomes, leading to personal growth and self-actualization.

While all this is true, these characteristics may not apply to everyone. Valuing these characteristics above all often prioritizes "me, my, mine" over "we, us, ours," which in the worst cases can create a society that places the needs of the privileged few above those of the wider world.

Is it possible that a new American ideal is evolving, despite much evidence to the contrary? Some people are embracing an ideal that emphasizes the notion that the welfare of individuals is interconnected and can be achieved through a collective effort. Some recognize the importance of social cohesion, mutual support, and shared responsibility for addressing societal issues.

Proponents argue that this new ideal promotes equality, social justice, and the redistribution of resources to ensure a more equitable society. It advocates for collaboration and cooperation, supportive and inclusive environments, social safety nets, and collective well-being.

Nothing is perfect. There is tension between the views. Critics of excessive individualism point out that it can lead to a fragmented society with weakened social bonds. But it's equally valid to say that undue emphasis on collective well-being can stifle individual initiative, personal freedoms, and creativity. At its most perilous, it can even lead to state control, limited personal autonomy, and the suppression of individual aspirations and dreams.

At best, rugged individualism and collective well-being are not opposing forces but complementary aspects of a thriving society. A more holistic approach acknowledges the importance of individual and personal responsibility, as well as the necessity of collective action, social support systems, and inclusive policies to ensure the well-being of all.

> The whole idea of compassion is based on a keen awareness of the interdependence of all these living beings, which are all part of one another and all involved in one another.
>
> *Thomas Merton*

MAPPING OUR STAGES OF GROWTH

We can reclaim the positive traits—the qualities of empathy, compassion, altruism, discernment, the loving generosity of our hearts—by understanding our inner development in the context of the stages of human development. Individualism is most beneficial when seen as one of many such stages. Developmental stages of growth have been scientifically mapped into steps or sequences. Just as a fruit-bearing tree goes through stages (seed, sapling, young, mature, and fruit-bearing), human maturation also progresses through stages, each new development including and transcending the previous one. In time, dependency grows into the capacity for independence, *not as the end goal but as a stage of development* that continues to unfold into a new capacity for interdependence. With maturity, both independence *and* interdependence are freely available.

Buddhist teacher and author Thich Nhat Hanh wrote in *The Art of Power*:

> It's like when you climb a ladder. When you get
> to the fourth rung, you may think you are on the
> highest step and cannot go higher, so you hold on
> to the fourth rung. But in fact there is a fifth rung;
> if you want to get to it, you have to be willing to
> abandon the fourth rung. Ideas and perceptions
> should be abandoned all the time, to make room
> for better ideas and truer perceptions. This is why
> we must always ask ourselves, "Am I sure?"[7]

As he suggests, we are standing on the rungs of a proverbial ladder—with one foot on the birthing level with its limited views of freedom. The other foot is reaching ahead, searching for the higher rung. For the ascending foot, old

---

7 Thich Nhat Hanh. *The Art of Power*. (New York: HarperCollins, 2007).

views feel stale, even harmful, less about freedom and more about willful blindness.

Rung by rung, our understanding deepens and broadens. Eventually, a new milestone of *interdependence* is achieved, and the idea of freedom opens up to a view, a dream of an interconnected world. Here, all are free, included, and unimpeded. Finally, we belong. Finally, we are home.

THE MISSING HEART OF MASLOW'S HIERARCHY OF NEEDS

Abraham Maslow's Hierarchy of Needs is well known. Since its introduction in the mid-20th century, it has provided a framework for understanding human motivation and the pursuit of self-actualization. I was introduced to it early in my training.

Maslow's Hierarchy of Needs is illustrated as a pyramid of five tiers: physiological needs, safety needs, love and belongingness needs, esteem needs, and self-actualization. According to Maslow, we must satisfy the lower-level needs before ascending to the higher ones, ultimately reaching self-actualization. For Maslow, the actualized self stands at the pinnacle of fulfillment.

Maslow's model has provided valuable insights into human motivation, although many have noted the limitations in Maslow's structure. Pointing out the complexity of human needs and aspirations, they argue that the idea that we must or can clearly satisfy each level before ascending to the next may be an oversimplification; that often we must juggle multiple needs simultaneously. Maslow's theory does not account for the impact of culture and society on individual needs and aspirations, or that self-actualization may be a primary, basic need in one culture but a higher-level need in another.

Limitations of Maslow's theory have spurred the emergence of alternative models. More recent work has illuminated the need for "self-transcendence," the importance of finding meaning in life that is beyond concerns for the self. In this conception, humans have an innate need and capacity to transcend themselves and connect with something greater through spirituality, creativity, or service to others.

And there's the work of Dr. Martin E.P. Seligman. His theory of well-being describes five building blocks and strategies to cultivate them. They are (1) positive emotions, (2) engagement, (3) relationships, (4) meaning, and (5) accomplishment. Sometimes called "positivity," applications of Seligman's theory have been criticized for denying, obscuring, or minimizing the existence or value of our human "not positive" or so-called "negative emotions." Newer models meant to transcend the limitations of "positivity" strive to be more inclusive and to promote a holistic view that embraces both light and shadow as ongoing, multidimensional processes.

THE HEARTFUL SCIENCE OF MIRROR NEURONS

In the 1990s, researchers at the University of Parma in Italy studied the part of the brain responsible for movement. In the study, monkeys were offered peanuts while hooked up to electrodes to monitor the activity of specific neurons. Each time the monkey picked up a peanut to eat, the monitor would click, click, click to signal neural activity.

One day, a researcher began to snack on a handful of peanuts. Click, click, click. Surprised, the researcher looked from the monitor to the monkey. What he saw was totally unexpected: As the monkey *watched* the researcher eat the peanuts, the area in his brain responsible for hand and mouth movement was lit up—yet the monkey was completely still. Since then, this experiment has been repeated numerous times with the same result. The neurons responsible for this empathic resonance with others are called "mirror neurons."

Mirror neurons are like emotional tuning forks. They fire both when we perform an action and when we witness someone else doing the same thing. This neural mirroring enables us to emotionally resonate with others, making it possible to share their joy, sadness, pain, or excitement. It is the neurological foundation of our capacity to understand and connect with fellow human beings on an emotional level.

Mirror neurons are thought to be the foundation of our capacity for deep empathy, bridging the gap between our own experiences and those of others, making us more compassionate and understanding individuals.

While the science of empathy helps us understand its biological and psychological roots, the *art* of empathy requires intention, presence, and vulnerability. It is the willingness to listen with an open heart, to suspend judgment, and to bear witness to another's truth without seeking to fix or change it. When we see someone else express an emotion, our mirror neurons fire, creating a shared experience. This shared lived experience is the basis of empathy—the ability to understand and feel what another person is feeling. It's that profound connection that says, "I see you. I feel you. You are not alone."

While I was writing this book, I adopted two cats when they were 12 years old. They had been together since birth; they were bonded. I had no heart to separate them, so I took them both. A couple of years later, one of them developed an aggressive tumor. He didn't have long to live. When his suffering reached a critical point, I made the difficult decision to euthanize him.

The vet and I euthanized him alone, and when the vet left, my neighbors came with me to the small plot where I had dug a grave. We sang a song together as I lowered him, wrapped in a kata, a scarf blessed by a Tibetan lama. Instead of a shovel, we gently filled his small grave with handfuls of garden soil. As the dirt fell from our hands and covered his tiny body, I saw tears in my neighbors' eyes. Their empathetic presence and compassion were comforting, a reminder that I was not alone.

A month earlier, I'd attended a FaceTime funeral for my niece, who lived in Canada. I couldn't make the trip, so I could only participate online. It was not the same as being together with my loved ones, although seeing and hearing them in that virtual space let me remember and grieve with my Canadian family. I'm grateful for the technology that made it possible.

As I reflected on the loss of my niece and then my cat, I was struck by how different these two experiences felt on a heart level. While I was grateful for the FaceTime funeral, I recall how, when we disconnected, I felt alone. My family was far away; I could not touch or hear them, hug or cry with them. I felt isolated, alone with my grief.

At that moment, I realized that the effortless convenience of online relationships doesn't allow love and caring to take hold. Physical presence has the potential to root profoundly and create supportive, life-affirming connections.

Empathy in its purest form is thought to go beyond mere cognitive awareness of the emotions and actions of others. As an *art*, empathy is an enactment of radical presence, a lived experience in which we are "at one with" others, while simultaneously differing in our unique joys and burdens.

DEEP EMPATHY IS A GAME-CHANGER

The concept of deep empathy makes a distinction between cognitively understanding another's perspective and a deeper emotional connection that allows us to "try on" what the other is experiencing much as we would if it were happening to us. Deep empathy challenges Maslow's outdated idea that we must solely focus on self-actualization and that reaching our personal highest potential is the ultimate goal. Instead, it reminds us that our highest potential is deeply intertwined with the well-being and happiness of others. It signals that our journey is not a solitary ascent to self-actualization but a collective voyage toward shared humanity.

That means we are not alone.

We have never been alone.

And never can be.

Deep empathy connects us to each other's joys, sorrows, and aspirations. We're not, and never have been, limited by our individuality, mere observers of the world around us. We're participants in a collective narrative, where the stories of others are also our own—and our own stories are woven into the fabric of a larger whole.

That means our humanity is not defined by what we achieve for ourselves, or our inner circle of family, but by how we engage with and uplift others. The kind of empathy that arises from mirror neurons is not just a soft skill that's nice to have; it's a fundamental aspect of our humanity that calls us to move beyond self-actualization and embrace collective actualization.

Deep empathy recognizes that the pursuit of personal growth and fulfillment must be accompanied by a commitment to the growth and well-being of our communities. It's no longer a simple pyramid but an interconnected web of needs and aspirations. The discovery of mirror neurons invites us to dismantle the hierarchy and recognize that true fulfillment lies in our ability to connect, empathize, and contribute to the well-being of others.

As we embody the heartful practice of deep empathy, we truly become something new, for it challenges our preconceptions, broadens our perspectives, and deepens our understanding of the world and our place in it, enabling us to become something greater—more compassionate, more connected, and more fully human. Empathy is one of the key practices that can help us reclaim our lost hearts and find our wholeness.

> Could a greater miracle take place than for us to look through each other's eyes for an instant?
>
> *Henry David Thoreau*

Heart Questions

1. What events in your life have felt like "high tides, flooding, and winds" that caused erosion in your heart's inner landscape? How might you nurture, cultivate, and reclaim the lost ground of your heart?

2. Reflect on a time in your life when you felt disconnected from others or your community. What steps did you take, or could you have taken, to reclaim a sense of belonging and interconnection?

3. How does empathy—given or received—show up in your life?

Chapter 5

Reclaiming Grief, Depression, and Loneliness

Story was the stuff of life, and to realise you
were inside one allowed you to sometimes
surrender to the plot, to bear a little easier
the griefs and sufferings and to enjoy more
fully the twists that came along the way.

Niall Williams, from This Is Happiness

———

WHEN WE IMMIGRATED, my mother was in her fifties. She had left her parents, nine siblings, numerous relatives, her privileged social role in the community, and the land, country, and language of her birth. There was little that she had not lost. Within two years of moving to Canada, she developed the colon cancer that eventually led to her death. She fell into a deep clinical depression.

Over time, I learned about depression and the many ways it is correlated with external and internal conditions. Depression is part of the processing of grief, just as anger, denial, and ultimately acceptance are part of the process (although not necessarily sequentially). Grief finds all of us. Even the most privileged among us will be visited by grief, by the loss of something or someone we love.

Grief is the aftermath of the experience of loss and a natural manifestation of our profoundly interconnected nature. When we lose someone or something we love, we feel wounded, like some part of ourselves has been ripped away. While we can learn to accept loss, the "myth of closure" is just that, a myth.

We each differ in how we respond to grief. Grief offers us a power to shut down or heal. We can hold grief close and make it part of our identity. It can become a story we repeat that sets us apart. Sometimes, it can become a means of feeling "other," "different," or special. It can disconnect us from others. It can also unite us through common experiences. No one escapes the experience of grief and loss.

In his sixties, decades after my mother died, my brother John had a stem cell transplant for multiple myeloma. (Years later, my brother Pete died of the same illness. My brothers had from an early age been exposed to toxins as they built gas stations all over Ontario.) John was the last patient in Ontario to have total body radiation, and in the years that followed, he was diagnosed with various cancers derived from the radiation. Especially hard for him was the neuropathy that was climbing up his legs.

A friend asked him, "John, you must be wondering, 'Why me, Lord?'"

John shrugged and shook his head, replying quietly, "Why *not* me?"

John did not consider himself to be remarkable. He was only one of many in the early days of transplants who'd suffered the fallout of total body radiation.

You could say John was stoic. I'm not sure that equates to unprocessed grief; for me, it is a different way of processing grief, a more internal, introverted, private process than the externalized, more public process of extroverts. In times of war, our American ideal way of grieving is, after all, not an available privilege. At such times, survival needs take priority over space for expressing personal emotions.

For nearly 50 years, Europeans did not speak of the war; only decades later did it become a subject of public discourse. The sometimes-beneficial self-dramatizing and self-identification with trauma fails to get an audience when everyone else has had the same experience.

Mental chatter can arise from reactive emotions like grief. The chatter tells us that things shouldn't be as they are, that life (or God) dealt us an unfair blow, that we didn't deserve this, or that we *did* deserve it and we are being rightfully punished. But these thoughts that spin around and around in our heads are learned strategies: Stories repeated over and over in our heads are much more tolerable and less painful than *feeling* the fragile vulnerability of grief.

A great loss has the potential of closing us down, walling us in, imprisoning us in a smaller and smaller world. You may know someone who has not left home in months or years due to grief. Or someone who no longer dares the risk of loving again.

Sometimes the luxury of grief must be delayed so that life can continue. Instead, life gets numb; the flames of emotions are dampened. Defenses shut down emotion's oxygen in the same way we can throw a shovelful of dirt on a campfire. Defenses can serve the purpose of survival as well as escape.

But a great loss also has the potential to open us up, to bring forth a depth of empathy and compassion never before available, and to connect us to others in ways that simply did not exist before. The key to staying connected during a time of loss is the willingness to accept "what is," to journey on, and to move through the grieving process without numbing out, shutting down, and lashing out.

We are social beings; our most profound suffering comes from loneliness and isolation, from the sense of *not belonging*. With physical pain, we know that the healing process is often more painful than the initial injury. Consider a broken bone that happens instantly against the long, painful path to recovery.

But with emotional pain, we are not rushed to the hospital to get our wounds stitched up, bones set, or sent to emergency surgery. With emotional pain, we are often surprised at the intensity of something we can neither see nor locate. One minute, our chest is too tight to breathe; the next, our stomach churns, and then burning sensations roll through us like deep ocean waves.

An entire year may go by, then another, and another. Life gets dull and then duller. A text in Buddhism reminds us that with physical injuries, there is a limit to how much pain the body can endure. But there seems to be no limit to the emotional pain, such as grief, a human can withstand. And no limit to how numb and lifeless our existence can become.

THE LONELY GRIEF OF COVID

During the second year of COVID, I recognized a neighbor at Trader Joe's. I'd been sheltering in place and hadn't seen Mary for two years. Even under her mask, she looked older than the years of absence would explain. I asked how she was doing. She looked down and then asked if I had a minute.

We finished shopping and met on a bench outside, open air, six feet apart. Mary was divorced and a single parent. I knew her kids and her family, so she felt comfortable with me.

She said she only had a few minutes; her sister was with the kids at home. When I asked after her mother, she looked down and quietly said she didn't make it. I waited for her to continue. After gathering herself, she explained that her mother, a widow who lived alone, had come down with COVID at the beginning of the pandemic before the vaccine was available. She was hospitalized, on a ventilator, and died two days later. Mary was not allowed in the hospital.

"Mom died alone," she said.

It broke my heart. During COVID, when I saw how the rituals of connecting that are so helpful in the healing process and which initiate involvement and support from family and friends were forbidden, it stirred memories of WWII when assisting Jews was forbidden. Resisters, at risk of their own lives, "disobeyed" and assisted anyway. Danger and risk are not limited to the physical threat of violence.

"I'm so sorry, Mary," I whispered.

We sat, wordless. Then, preparing to leave, I asked about the kids and her job. She stood up and looked at me over her shoulder as she gathered her bags. "I lost my job. Working part-time now. And homeschooling. It's driving us all nuts."

I glanced at her shopping cart and wondered how she could make ends meet. She waved and drove off quickly. I knew where she lived and knew I would stop by. We could meet outside if we must.

My visit with Mary in the Trader Joe's parking lot stuck with me for several days. The circumstances of COVID were triggering flashbacks of choices made in WWII. Not all laws must be obeyed. Moral choices and political rules are not always in alignment.

The only way to survive is by taking care of one another.

Grace Lee Boggs

BEING A WITNESS TO GRIEF

When the 2004 Indian Ocean tsunami hit Southeast Asia, it was Christmas Day, and I was with my sister. We saw the news on TV. It was automatic for me, as I thought, *I've got to go. I've got to help.* Nelly knew me well, asking, "You're not going, are you?"

Grief can either open or close our hearts.

Colleagues in my practice supported and covered for me. I took a few days to make appropriate connections for my vulnerable clients so that they would be well cared for and in informed hands during my absence. Several days later, suitcases maxed out with supplies from various organizations and private individual donors and friends, I flew out as a volunteer in a private catastrophe relief group.

In Sri Lanka, connections were made with an orphanage, a hospital, and women leaders in their villages. I shared what I had learned in my training with Elisabeth Kübler-Ross, my work with the then-named Coalition for Terminal Care, my experience drafting medical school curriculum for a class in end-of-life care, and my participation in establishing the initial hospice program in Minneapolis.

Days after the tsunami, I sat with children in a shelter in Sri Lanka. They had lived on the shores of the sea and played in the surf their entire lives. They were now afraid of the water. A man who lost 13 family members stood overwrought with fear when his remaining child, 11 years old, disappeared to use the toilet. I stood in a field surrounded by women village leaders. Most were numb, feeling neither grief nor fear. All were in shock, their minds no longer processing what their eyes were seeing.

Every day, the women reached out quietly, walked with me on the empty shores that had held homes and villages, and sat beside me in the fields. We joined with local people to rebuild homes and a community shelter. We had brought medicine, supplies for dental care, and other resources.

They said that our presence told them that people in my country shared the grief of Sri Lankans.

On many days, I would sit with them at sundown. All I could do was stay close, sit quietly beside them, encourage them, pray with them, and take their hand if they offered it.

DEPRESSION CAN BE A TUNING FORK

How does one sit with people during grief or depression and not over-identify with or succumb to their emotions? How do we cultivate compassion for our self and others without taking on their suffering as our own?

It was an October midmorning when Jennie walked into my office. She briefly summarized that she was married with two kids, her husband was gainfully employed, and they had an okay marriage. "I'm a high school music teacher," she added. When I asked how I could help, she looked down, her hands in her lap. I was aware of a sudden shift of mood in the room and me; I realized she was exuding a powerful, quiet sadness that permeated the air around her.

"I'm depressed," she said. "My physician prescribed meds but said I should see someone."

When I asked her to tell me something about herself so that I would better understand the context of her life circumstances, she said she was the eldest of 10 children. "It might be genetic," she explained; as I lifted my eyebrows, she smiled and added, "I grew up in the shadow of my mother's depression!" I asked her to say more about that, and she said, "It's like a tuning fork!"

I was admittedly perplexed. There had been a stark absence of music education in my early life, so the metaphor went by me. (We sang hymns and patriotic songs around the organ, but no music education.) I asked her to elaborate, and she painted a poignant image of the phenomenon of sympathetic resonance, where a vibrating tuning fork induces vibrations in another of the same frequencies when brought close by. She was describing a way she believed that her depression may have been transmitted by proximity. Could close contact with someone consumed by sadness, anger, or intense emotion awaken those feelings in a mutual resonance?

Her metaphor stayed with me and provided a fresh, powerful analogy that spoke to the potentially contagious nature of emotions within family relationships.

That evening, alone at home, I reflected on the subtle ways my father, mother, and siblings' emotional states may have saturated my childhood moods and perceptions. Even now, early life memories remain, haunting reminders of the power and lasting impact of those experiences.

In my childhood, I was attuned to my father. He did not speak of it, but I had tuned into the heaviness of his burdens. I understood what it might have been like for him to witness his wife's illness and depression and watch one of his daughters dive into insanity. I wanted to be a support for him.

As patriarch, he was responsible for the family's move from Holland. He bore witness to my mother's suffering—cancer, colostomy, her shame, and isolation. For his daughter, who was sentenced by a psychiatrist to confinement to a state hospital, he bore witness to her torture of shock treatments and insulin shocks. I have an idea of what his choice cost him.

He lived with the choice and impact of migrations: the grief of living far away, learning by letter of the death of his siblings and parents, all in Holland while he was far away in Canada. There were no available funds to allow him to travel back.

I recognized his quiet grief, the daily practice of letting go in the face of overwhelming losses: of family, identity, societal status, financial security, and respect. His years after migration were confined to the struggle to keep us fed, clothed, and sheltered.

He'd sought a better future in the wilderness, but hardship followed. The accumulation of loss had been staggering. The gains came only many years later, and those losses were never balanced. The story of most of the first generations of migrants.

I tried to comfort my father; I experienced his restrictions, despite his brilliance and his potential. I sensed a flicker of his unfulfilled dreams in my own life. My travels and exploration of the world may have been a way of living out his unfulfilled dreams, an echo of adventures and experiences he longed for but couldn't pursue as the eldest of 13, burdened by responsibility for his own family as strangers in a strange land.

Clinicians learn from their clients, and Jennie was a teacher. Her work impacted me, opened my awareness, and deepened my realizations. I hear her words, "the power of emotional contagion," as I learn from researchers now studying how emotions can spread through our social connections, empathy, mirror neurons, and automatic mimicry.[8] Complex conditions such as depression, anxiety, and loneliness, even

---

8 Lisiê Valéria Paz, Thiago Wendt Viola, Bruna Bueno Milanesi, Juliana Henz Sulzbach, Régis Gemerasca Mestriner, Andrea Wieck, and Léder Leal Xavier, "Contagious Depression: Automatic Mimicry and the Mirror Neuron System—A Review," *Neuroscience & Biobehavioral Reviews* 134 (2022): 104509, https://doi.org/10.1016/j. neubiorev.2021.12.032.

discontent, are thought to be "catching," spread to family members, close friends, partners, roommates, and coworkers. Others are exploring a genetic connection, noting that longitudinal studies have shown that children of parents with a history of major depressive episodes are four to ten times more likely than other children to develop major depression.[9]

Perhaps we all live out some part of our parents and family bonds in quiet, undramatic ways, continuing to humor, amaze, and revolt against each other even across time, generations, and vast distances.

As a clinician, I became acquainted with how quickly depression can lead to emotional numbness, disconnection, and withdrawal, a state where feelings are guarded and vulnerability is avoided.

I witnessed how depression restricts the ability to experience joy, the pleasure of connecting. I saw how the heart shuts down as the subjective experience of the world as gray and devoid of meaning leaves little room for the experience of love or joy.

I walked with many who were overcoming depression. I've witnessed the process of once again opening emotionally, allowing oneself to feel and connect, to embrace life's vulnerability, to open to accepting and allowing the presence of love and support.

---

9   William R. Beardslee, Martin B. Keller, Philip W. Lavori, Janet Staley, and Natalie Sacks, "The Impact of Parental Affective Disorder on Depression in Offspring: A Longitudinal Follow-up in a Nonreferred Sample," Journal of the American Academy of Child & Adolescent Psychiatry 32, no. 4 (1993): 723–730, https://doi.org/10.1097/00004583-199307000-00004.

I've witnessed the change that comes as self-compassion and acceptance increase. The energizing power as a kinder, more loving relationship with oneself amplifies.

As a gardener, I see it much like a flower opening its bud to the light of the sun—a reopening of the heart as the light of self-love and forgiveness blooms, renews, and energizes.

The visual metaphor of an open/closed heart captures the emotional and relational aspects of depression. It goes beyond the purely cognitive or biological explanations and speaks to the core human need for connection and love, offering a hopeful vision of healing. By opening our hearts, we can find a way out of the darkness of depression and reconnect with the world as we reconnect with lost or dormant aspects of who we are.

Healing from depression can be likened to reclaiming the heart. When we are depressed, we may lose touch, shut down, or get lost in the tone of a mood, of existential meaninglessness. The heart can feel stolen, locked away. Coming out of depression can feel like thawing from numbness. As the heart heals, it's as if there is a "click" when we are again surprised by joy, enlivened by connection, and are willing to open again to the joys and sorrows of life. We once again feel eager to experience "the flow" and fullness of energy, the vitality of being alive. As a sense of well-being returns, the heart reclaims a connection, a flow of compassion, and the amity to enter the dance of tension, of vulnerability and authenticity.

LONELINESS

A Meta-Gallup study in 2023 called *The Global State of Social Connections* found that nearly a quarter (24%) of adults globally experience significant loneliness, with 10% experiencing it daily. The report also names that loneliness and social isolation have proven links to chronic health conditions, such as hypertension, diabetes, dementia, and cardiovascular disease, as well as depression and anxiety, which are associated with an elevated risk of premature death. In 2024, a poll by the American Psychiatric Association (APA) revealed that 30% of American adults report feeling lonely at least weekly in the past year.

Thomas Oppong, in his blog on Medium, shared an insight by Carl Jung that some people are lonely not because they don't have people around, but because they are unable to communicate the things that seem important, or particular views others don't want to hear.[10] I resonate with what Jung wrote in his autobiography, *Memories, Dreams, Reflections*:

> As a child, I felt alone, and I am still [alone]
> because I know things and must hint at things
> that others know nothing of and, for the most
> part, do not want to know.[11]

Oppong unpacks Jung's ideas about loneliness further, how loneliness speaks to a profound sense of disconnection. We might define connection as relationships where we can share our inner thoughts and feelings, the things that truly matter to us. For some of us, that means recipes or football games. For others, it's abstract or creative ideas. Most of us withdraw into

---

10 Thomas Oppong, "Carl Jung's Unsettling Truth Explains Why People Get Lonely," Medium, May 30, 2024, https://medium.com/personal-growth/carl-jungs-unsetting-truth-on-why-people-get-lonely-56ce6084b31f.

11 C.G. Jung, Memories, Dreams, Reflections, rev. ed., rec. and ed. Aniela Jaffé, trans. Richard and Clara Winston (New York: Vintage, 1989).

ourselves when we feel unheard, unseen, unknown, or misunderstood. Loneliness sets in, even when we are surrounded by people. When our sense of self, beliefs, and perspectives are considered unacceptable or of no interest, the gulf of silence separates us from each other. It's not that we are physically alone; when expressing ourselves is not welcomed, we are cut off from communicating and sharing our inner lives. The sense of acceptance and belonging is not present.

THE DANGERS OF DISCONNECTING

People divorced from community, occupation,
and association are first and foremost
among the supporters of extremism.

Robert Putnam

In his 2000 book *Bowling Alone*, Robert D. Putnam addresses human disconnection. Through fine detail and a wealth of research, he explains how we've become so disconnected. His message is brilliantly summarized in two words: bowling alone. These two simple words conjure up images from our not-so-distant past, when coming together in cheerful and relaxed fellowship was familiar—a reminder of something lost.

When a deep sense of connectedness and belonging is lost, bowling alone can become much more than simple loneliness or personal health—it can also pose an emerging threat to society.

Putnam's 2020 book with Shaylyn Romney Garrett, *The Upswing*, paints a compelling picture of how today's increase in loneliness is directly tied to social isolation that has grown with the decline of community engagement. They reiterate the devastating impact of loneliness

on individuals, citing not only the physical health problems it can cause but also the psychological toll it takes.
Putnam starkly notes that loneliness can be as harmful to
one's health as obesity or smoking, echoing the U.S. Surgeon General warnings about the increased risks of anxiety,
depression, and suicide known to be associated with feelings of isolation and non-belonging.[12]

Putnam and Garrett further explore the broader social
and political ramifications of loneliness, arguing that it
erodes social trust, diminishes civic participation, and frays
the very fabric of our communities. They even link loneliness
to the rise of political polarization and extremism, suggesting that when people feel disconnected, they become more
susceptible to divisive rhetoric and less open to considering
opposing viewpoints.

The Upswing sounds a powerful call to action. It reminds
me to be cautious of how advertisements lure us into "conveniences" that relieve us of needing each other: we can
have our own cars, our own house, exercise equipment, and
movies, and soon our own robots to watch our elderly. It
reminds us of the importance of mobilizing to reverse these
trends. Like the late Minnesota Senator Paul Wellstone,
Putnam and Garrett underscore that "we all do better when
we all do better." Social connections, community, and civic
engagement are important tasks and tools for us as individuals as well as for the greater good.

I'll never forget what my father told me about neighbors and
members of the Resistance. "In the Occupation, you never

---

12 Vivek Murthy, *Together: The Healing Power of Human Connection in a
Sometimes Lonely World*, (New York: Harper Wave, 2020).

knew who would be brave. Men considered brave broke within a few hours of interrogation, named names, and divulged plans." He went on, "Just as often, men who were considered cowards before the war died rather than betray the Resistance or their Jewish neighbors." Neighbors who were community leaders betrayed others for a loaf of bread or to ensure safety.

"You couldn't predict it," he added.

I took his point: It's complex, trying to understand how we view ourselves and others—and why we connect or disconnect.

NEIGHBORS ARE AN ANTIDOTE TO LONELINESS

I have lived in my Minneapolis neighborhood of Linden Hills for 40-plus years. I know my neighbors. I've watched generations of children grow up, and I have seen neighborhood elderly move and die. Like other octogenarians, I lived before television—when evenings were filled with voices of kids playing skip rope on the sidewalks, riding bicycles, or casting "jacks" on the front porch.

Things have changed. Doors to the porch are now more often closed, and the light inside shines on families sitting side by side on couches, watching TV or scrolling on their phones. How, in these times, do we maintain that significant, essential neighborly connection?

I had a small idea that blossomed: I opened my garage to community gatherings. People connected, had ideas. Here are some of the magical things I saw happen:

Locally renowned musician-neighbors playing in the driveway, surrounded by families singing together. A father leading a group of neighbors (lots of kids!) as we sang and gestured along to "The Wheels on the Bus." A young neighbor performing "Smoke on the Water" on his handmade dulcimer. A group of young girls showing off their dribbling skills to honor Caitlin Clark. Magic tricks, hula-hooping, piano recital selections shared, poems read, stories told, and many choruses of "Puff the Magic Dragon" sung. Neighbors introducing themselves, pulling out more chairs. A neighbor garden tour followed by refreshments and visiting. A plan for Halloween: permission to close the street to make it safe and great for kids and families. Fresh vegetables delivered from a neighbor's farm. Careful planning for Neighborhood Night Out . . . an atmosphere that went deep into the evening. Neighbors stringing holiday lights between homes, the metaphor of connection. The gift of attendance: If someone throws a ball and no one catches it, there is no game! Shoveling snow for each other. Going out of the way to provide an "in-person" welcome to new arrivals on the block. Picking up bagels for each other. During COVID, neighbors offering their help to those who could not shop for themselves. A call for shopping bags to be used to collect food so it wouldn't be wasted. Neighbors and kids chatting together, playing together, getting to know one another.

I later learned that four blocks away, a neighbor had started a garden in his backyard. Each spring, they invited children and their parents to plant seeds, tending the garden through summer and harvesting and eating together in autumn.

There is great power in neighborhoods. In gathering and relating, we the people really are the foundation of democracy. We can't individually stop the bombing in Gaza and Lebanon, but we all have the power of small things, and caring is never small. It is contagious.

All experiences that become accomplishments in time start small, in small moments, small openings that are recognized as opportunities. I opened my garage door, and neighbors gathered.

Nurture strength of spirit to shield you in sudden misfortune. But do not distress yourself with dark imaginings. Many fears are born of fatigue and loneliness.

Max Ehrmann

Heart Questions

1. When have you chosen to accompany someone in their grief, or had someone do so for you?

2. How would you describe your core needs and how you meet them (or not)?

3. Who or what is your community? How does your community evolve with your life experience?

Chapter 6

Transforming Anger and Shame

One does not become enlightened
by imagining figures of light, but by
making the darkness conscious.

Carl G. Jung

———

EMOTIONS DRIVE THE narratives of our lives: as primal forces, they can shape our thoughts, inform our decisions, and, ultimately, mold our destinies. Our emotions have impact beyond ourselves, even if we're unaware of those consequences.

Emotions also play a significant role in shaping the larger societal landscape. Collective emotions have the potential to spark social movements and provoke profound transformations within society. In my mind, this is why community organizing is so important. When communities come together to share a common emotion, such as anger over injustices or the exhilaration of achieving a collective goal, it becomes a catalyst for change, potentially reshaping our communities and social norms.

However, emotions can also be unsettling, divisive, and disruptive forces. To confront our emotions head-on is to engage the shadow self—aspects of ourselves we suppress or deny. This confrontation can be a painful yet essential step toward growth.

Often called "negative emotions," hatred and fear can easily be weaponized and exploited by individuals or groups to manipulate and polarize societies. They are present in the re-emergence of white supremacists, neo-Nazis, and conspiracy theorists, to name of few that have infected American culture of late. Their presence is a stark reminder that our emotions have power. They can shape our thoughts, inform our decisions, and mold our destinies. Negative emotions are also a call to action, reminding us of the need for heightened awareness, understanding, and emotional intelligence at both the individual and societal levels.

> One can only face in others what
> one can face in oneself.
>
> *James Baldwin*

WHEN OUR PAST COLORS OUR FUTURE

When I was a child, I had a bad case of pneumonia and bronchitis. Evidence of those illnesses remains in my lungs. In the same way, I carry the shadow of WWII emotional experiences in my heart and mind, which influences my view today. In post-COVID America, as I witness the degree of racism and hate crimes prevalent today, it occurs to me that Americans may underestimate the wildfire potential of fear and hate. Very few have firsthand remembrance of the Nazi wildfire of the 1930s, the propaganda storm that unleashed the war in the 1940s and lit the torch that normalized what was once unthinkable.

We know that empathy can spread through a community. We also know that hatred and aggression can do the same. Like a virus, anger and hatred can infect everyone they touch. While I yearn to think of the Dutch people as pure and above the atrocities committed by the Nazis in Germany, this was not the case. Like racist Americans and anti-immigrant forces everywhere, Dutch anti-Semites willingly took part in the stigmatization of their Jewish neighbors and countrymen.

Anger gives way to open discrimination, then hate, then hate crimes.

Propaganda campaigns, which depicted Jews as vermin, began in Europe in the 1930s, well before the invasion of Holland. Before the Nazi occupation, there were only Dutch people in my little village. After Germany invaded and defeated Holland overnight, there were Dutch people and Jewish people.

During the occupation of Holland, some people collaborated, seeking favor with the Nazis by informing on the Resistance, on Jews, and even those who were "Jew friendly." You could receive extra rations, like a loaf of bread, in exchange for the address of a Jew. Being known as a Jew-hater or collaborating against the Resistance guaranteed a measure of privilege and safety. Being labeled a Jew sympathizer guaranteed an equal measure of peril.

Ambiguity, doubt, and uncertainty became the air people breathed. Neighbors turned against neighbors. Slowly, inconspicuously, the scapegoating began. Jews were forced to wear a yellow star on their chests. Yellow stars were dodged on the streets, and mere proximity became increasingly dangerous. Fear morphed into hatred. Long-held associations were broken. As Aryan purification stepped up, silos tightened, and Holland became a country divided.

In the tight box of village life, little was private. Everyone knew who was Jewish and who was not. It took extraordinary courage and deep inner conviction to remain true to your values when survival fear ran so high.

In the Bible story about the exodus of Israel from Egypt, there's the phrase, "Pharaoh hardened his heart." The heart is not just sugar and spice, as some would like to believe. It makes choices. Voters make choices. Donald Trump has a heart and makes choices. So did Mother Teresa, who was capable of her own kind of strangeness. If it was not so, being good and making choices would be easy, but often that's not the case. It's costly and requires sacrifice of some kind—sometimes more, sometimes less; too much for some, not too great for others.

EMOTIONS DEFINE OUR CHOICES

During and after the Occupation, Dutch people used fear to justify their choices. There was no question about the reality of the danger. Association with Jews, like associating with someone infected by COVID, was dangerous, even life-threatening—not only for you but for your entire family.

Emotions drive choices. I spoke with a friend recently who was raised in the South in the 1950s and '60s. "It was dangerous to mix freely with Black people then," he said. "The KKK was powerful, and you never knew who would turn you in and who wouldn't. Your safety and your family's safety depended on who you knew, associated with, and condemned."

I'm shaped by my history. I remember the 1960s and the choices I made. The college campuses of America were filled with many forms of resistance to the war, racism, and sexism, as well as activism for human rights. Some of my friends resisted the draft by fleeing to Canada. My own life had been saved by Canadian soldiers who liberated Holland from the Nazis. More friends went to jail for refusing to go to Vietnam. I protested the war, was tear-gassed, hit by police on Telegraph Hill, and "busted" at a protest at the induction center. It was a time of sorting out ambiguous emotions and shaping my own true north of values. Today, a Vietnam veteran with dementia spends weekends at my home. He is a dear friend.

During the pandemic, I once again was triggered. This time, what "set me off" was knowing of people who were alone, in isolation. As a psychologist, I knew the impact of isolation on the immune system. I knew the psychological stress of being abandoned to deal with danger alone. I remembered how the Geneva Convention deemed isolation as torture. For me, those left without pods of connection were the "Jews" of the pandemic.

I felt an intense impulse to help the isolated; I was somehow willing to take careful personal risks to reach out. I did not understand the public's indifference—the way personal safety canceled concern for others, for those who lived alone, the elderly and most vulnerable. I read how the Canadian health department was encouraging people to include them into family pods. It threw me back to the war when sheltering the vulnerable was also life-threatening. I remembered the call to resistance.

It reminded me of the painful, dangerous choices people I knew had made in childhood. I remembered the resisters and the collaborators. I remembered soldiers who risked their lives, aid workers in war zones. I thought of our military, of those who heal and care for the wounded, the hurting and dying. Of firefighters, of those who raced up the Twin Towers on September 11, 2001. Few of my friends understood my urgency. They had not gone through the war of my childhood experience. History can define us, explaining what we see as possible choices. Our choices, in turn, define us.

One day during the pandemic, I felt anger and surprise arising when an elderly veteran, a nearby neighbor whose son was stationed overseas, stopped to greet me as he walked by my house with his Springer spaniel. I asked how he was, and he spoke of being alone. His friends had receded into family pods, while he, a recent widower, spent long days alone. Now in his eighties and vision impaired, he was not able to access the new Zoom, nor could he attend church services online. He understood that friends didn't want to take risks. I was not so understanding. We found ways to safely socially distance by meeting outside, where we drank hot chocolate while wrapped in blankets under an outdoor patio heater I had purchased.

Few saw the pandemic isolation as I saw it. We were looking through different lenses. It left me feeling alone, doubting my own sanity. I called my sister for support and confirmation. I reflected on my choices and renewed my values. A local newspaper[13] picked up my idea of forming pods for the isolated. My colleague Brenda Hartman, a clinical social worker, and I coined a new term for those isolated during the pandemic—SILOS: Single Individuals Left Out of Society.

Our emotions have tremendous power over us. Relationships rise and fall on the expression of feelings. We take

---

13 Gail Rosenblum, "Twin Cities Therapists Emphasize Need to Prepare Purposeful COVID 'Bubbles' Before Winter," *Minnesota Star Tribune*, September 25, 2020, https://www.startribune.com/ twin-cities-therapists-emphasize-need-to-prepare-purposeful-covid- bubbles-before-winter/572522061.

great risks to avoid embarrassment and shun great opportunities to avoid the shame of failure. Emotions can wound and overwhelm us. There is some evidence that a "broken heart" can be more than metaphorical, that it can injure the physical heart beyond repair. Many of us are so afraid of our emotions that suicide seems to be the only way out. Uncompromising emotions left unchecked can limit our choices, drive our decisions, and may even drive us to the brink of psychosis.

A current experience can trigger contact with an emotional experience of a past event and "set us off." Unguarded emotions can put a public face on our inner world.

Emotions occur quickly. So quickly that we often feel like helpless victims, as if we are not the agents of our own thoughts and actions. In the wake of a strong emotion, intervention seems impossible.

ANGER LEADS TO HATRED

A man said to Buddha, "I look at you and see a dirty pig."
The Buddha replied, "I look at you and see a Buddha."

Hate, exemplified by the above comment to Buddha, is an extreme emotional position driven by relentless, irrational, and merciless anger. Viewing the world through a prism of hate has created immeasurable suffering in the world. According to renowned teacher and author Jack Kornfield, anger, hatred, and aggression are universal energies that push against the reality of the present moment.

These universal energies directly react to a perceived threat, injustice, or cruelty. They can cause a person to become so filled with hate that he sees someone as vermin or looks at the Buddha and sees a dirty pig.

When propaganda, peer pressure, or other cultural/personal forces blind us to the humanity of other people, it's easier to view them with anger, hate, and contempt. We see them as things, what some call "thingifying." Sir Terry Pratchett, in his novel *I Shall Wear Midnight*, astutely wrote, "Evil begins when you begin to treat people as things." Anger can lead to extremes, to polarization, a dualizing that opens the door to what Karl Marx referred to as *Verdinglichung*, which literally means "making into a thing" in German and represents a process that dehumanizes and rationalizes violence.

In the short but powerful book *I and Thou* (1923), Martin Buber refers to this process when describing our relationship with others as twofold. For him, the I-Thou relationship is a "sacred" encounter with the other as a whole person with inherent worth, while in an I-It relationship, we perceive the other as an object, a thing, or a means to an end. Buber writes:

> If I face a human being as my *Thou*, and say the
> primary word *I–Thou* to him, he is not a thing
> among things, and does not consist of things.[14]

In no way naïve, Buber acknowledges the shadow impulses that live in us all and suggests what mindset can overcome thinking of people as things: "[Since] we cannot avoid using power, cannot escape the compulsion to afflict the world, so let us, cautious and mighty in contradiction, love powerfully."

----

14 Martin Buber, *I and Thou*, repr. ed., trans. Ronald Gregor Smith (Edinburgh: T. & T. Clark, 1952).

The heart can open, it can close. It can harden, it can soften. These ideas have long been with us. It's true that anger can lead to hatred—but the choice is always ours.

> The human heart is a dark, unyielding mystery. It is a perforated jug with a mouth forever open; though all rivers of the earth pour in, it will remain empty and thirsting. The greatest of hopes had not filled it. Would it be filled now by the greatest of despairs? (Report to Greco)
>
> *Nikos Kazantzakis*

WHEN ANGER TAKES A STAND

What about the other side of anger, which says no to injustice; resists norms, orders, and rules; and uses the power of emotions to take a stand?

Here again, I think of conversations with my father.

From him I learned there must be dividing lines, boundaries, that must not be crossed. "There are some roads love won't take," he said frequently. "And some things you may not permit. There are times when you must resist. When non-resistance becomes participation by enabling."

Participation in the Resistance defined and clarified his values. During the Occupation, neutrality was not an option. "You must act. To remain silent, to put your head in the sand, or throw up your hands in overwhelm is to be complicit. There is just as much risk in complacency as in outright rebellion," he said.

For him, anger was not to be expressed as rage, as unregulated, boiled-up fury. He deemed such anger foolish, neither just, productive, nor humane. He spoke often of his friend, Jan van Wagenaar, who was imprisoned then executed by the Nazis. Not only was Jan shot, but his son was shot with him. During times of war, there is no certainty, no place to hide. All you have abides in your heart. Complacency protects no one.

Opportunities to resist are available to us in life today. It takes various forms, from making conscious choices—like consuming products that that are ethically sourced, that don't inflict cruelty on animals, are not made at someone's expense—to choices that respect our environment and reduce harm. Resistance can be voting, engaging in peaceful protests, civil disobedience, and supporting causes that promote dignity and respect, justice and equality for all. We all need an internal ethical ground to hold ourselves against.

SHAME IS A MORAL COMPASS

Shame is an unspoken epidemic, the secret
behind many forms of broken behavior.

Brené Brown

For many people worldwide, shame is a feeling we experience when we don't live up to expectations or fall short of our potential. Shame tells us that our actions do not suit the good person we hold ourselves to or the person we want to be.

As a moral compass, shame expresses disappointment in one's choices and behavior. We all need an internal ethical ground, a strong inner voice that says: *I stand here. And I will not be moved.* Shame, as an internal moral compass, is about holding that ground, feeling regret about our behavior when we fail to be faithful to our values.

It may sound counterintuitive, but as a moral compass, shame can unite a culture by upholding normative, commonly accepted values. When someone betrays these values, it registers as a feeling, a dark betrayal of trust.

Shame can be weaponized. In WWII, those who didn't meet the Aryan ideal were likened to vermin, efficiently destroyed. Such shaming, though underground, lives on today. When weaponized and wielded with the intent of controlling another, shame has the power to suffocate and divide, to undermine our instinct to connect with others. When internalized, weaponized shame knows no boundaries.

This sinister side of shame is not guilt. Shame does not prod us to recognize and take responsibility for our mistakes as guilt does. Shame targets our very being—it attacks our sense of self. It whispers insidious lies that we are unworthy, flawed, and undeserving of love and belonging. Shame convinces us that we are alone in our suffering, rendering us vulnerable to its torment.

When shame cuts too deeply, when it is wielded with a heavy hand and the intent to harm rather than guide, it can leave emotional scars that manifest as a permanent sense of self-loathing and create an impenetrable wall of isolation.

For example, kids learn by trial and error; we all make mistakes. Mistakes are choices. Kids feel their parents' attitudes about their "mistakes" but cannot yet distinguish the guiding direction of those attitudes. Skillful parents clearly distinguish between approval and disapproval of their child's behavior and their child's being. "I love you. You are my good boy, but taking your sister's toy is not okay! You must give it back," is a different message than "You took your sister's toy; you are a bad boy."

Persistent anxiety and perpetual insecurity suffered by adults can often be traced back to a humiliating experience in childhood. Even toddlers imagine what others think of them. With repeated expressions of disappointment by a caretaker, children experience a sense of insecurity and isolation.

Sexual abuse, domestic abuse, and drug addiction are all associated with shame. To be publicly shamed affects every aspect of a person's life: their sense of self-worth, sense of dignity, and ability to form intimate relationships. Shame can cripple, can undermine one's ability to keep a job or get a promotion. Shame is the most accessible and lethal weapon one person can wield against another. And in today's world, it is wielded frequently and shamelessly.

A CAPTURED HEART:
THE CHAIN OF EMOTIONAL REACTIVITY

When a strong reactive emotion like anger or shame is triggered, it often feels like we've been hit by a rogue wave that we didn't even see coming. And yet, studies have shown that even our strongest emotions unfold linearly—more like the links in a chain than a wall of roiling water.

And like a chain, emotions progress along a continuum, having a beginning, middle, and end. During this time of heightened emotions, we may experience mental fog, emotional confusion, and mild irritation, only to suddenly erupt into a turmoil of destructive emotions. We may interpret an innocent remark as a personal attack, which initiates the last phase: our stress response. The immediate reaction may range from an angry tirade (fight) to timid withdrawal (flight) to an inability to express our thoughts (freeze).

A self-aware heart can respond, but a captured heart reacts. *How* we react is determined by our conditioned beliefs. Perhaps we believe life should not be as it is; we were dealt an unfair blow. We didn't deserve this! Or someone else is to blame, and they should be punished. Or perhaps we believe we deserved it and should be punished even more. Past conditioning can distort our ability to think clearly, making it difficult to respond appropriately.

How can we deal with reactive emotions? While each spiritual tradition has its own nuances of expression, and the specific practices differ, there is general agreement on the antidotes for reactive emotions. All spiritual traditions encourage:

- seeking out connection and guidance through the support of spiritual companions, while promoting spiritual practices like meditation, prayer, non-judgmental awareness, and emotional self-regulation

- activating the power of compassion and forgiveness as a heart-opening means of releasing anger and resentment

- cultivating ethical conduct and virtues such as restraint, patience, forgiveness, and mercy

Not everyone has access to these skills and capacities, however. When we are captured by a triggered emotion—which can last hours, days, months, or even years—we keep rehashing the painful event. New information is blocked out. We allow only thoughts that reinforce the original emotional reaction.

However intense and destructive our conditioned reactivity becomes, we are not helpless victims. Intervention is possible because emotions tend to unfold in predictable ways. Here's an example of a sudden intense emotion that eventually settles into a dark, unshakeable mood.

"I'm in a bad mood," you confide to a friend.

"Why?" comes the response.

"Some jerk flipped me off on the highway. He yelled at me for a mile."

"When did it happen?"

A mood can last for an hour, a day, or maybe a few days. Moods influence how we think, making us vulnerable to sudden emotional swings. When we are in a bad mood, we quickly become annoyed. We look for opportunities to become angry.

But if it continues, it is no longer just a mood; it becomes a *temperament*. Then, people describe you as hot-tempered, irritable, or rigid to work with. After a while, the temperament becomes a character trait. You don't even notice it anymore. "It's just who I am," you say.

Now, let's look at another example, replacing anger with fear. Say you were in the grocery store when someone approached you frighteningly and aggressively. You were trembling when you got to your car. For days afterward, you were shaky and tearful. You can't stop reliving the experience in your mind. Your mood is dark as night.

You begin to avoid that grocery store even though it means driving further. You may even avoid all grocery stores, choosing delivery instead. Then, a deep sense of dread about all public places sets in. You put double locks on your doors. You refuse invitations from your friends. You have become a recluse, lonely and filled with paralyzing fear.

Predictably, you have been captured; your heart and mind are chained to some event from the past.

Let it go. Let it out. Let it all unravel. Let it free
and it can be a path on which to travel.

Michael Leunig

DISSOLVING THE ARMOR THAT SHEATHS THE HEART

Like a protective cocoon or the shell of a seed that allows it to survive the harshness of winter, the heart's armor protects us from potential wounds. The armor emerges from many sources—fragile self-esteem, societal norms, past traumas, fears of rejection, and the relentless pressure to conform. It manifests in various forms—in defenses, like the masks we wear in our relationships and the barriers we construct to protect our innermost vulnerabilities. There are two sides to defenses; while they may protect us from potential harm, they also limit the possibility of authentic connections, preventing us from fully experiencing the richness of life and relationships.

Heart armor, while initially comforting, can become a prison. Built from the bricks of anger, shame, and fear, it can insulate and isolate us from our true selves.

The cost of keeping ourselves hidden is high.

We trade the richness of authenticity for the illusion of safety. We forfeit the chance to connect with others profoundly, and we settle for superficial interactions that leave our hearts unfulfilled. The cost may be the distance it creates between us and the intimate connections that form the richness of life.

Dissolving these "armoring" patterns requires a profound shift in our perspective, an inner pilgrimage toward the heart of our own being. We open ourselves up to the transformative power of authenticity by unveiling our true selves. In shared vulnerability, we discover the common threads that unite us, the grace of deep connections and love.

However, let's acknowledge that it's not always safe in every circumstance, in every life, to be vulnerable—such as in the workplace if there is not "psychological safety." Harvard Business School professor Amy Edmondson and author of *The Fearless Organization* coined the term "psychological safety." It means a workplace environment where people feel comfortable sharing ideas, questions, concerns, and mistakes without fear of punishment or humiliation.[15] Behavioral scientist Carey Yazeed challenges the idea that psychological safety happens on a level playing field. Expecting employees to be vulnerable isn't feasible in situations where a person of color or a woman might then be viewed as weak, with repercussions regarding job advancement. Yazeed writes:

> Before a person of any race can begin to embrace vulnerability and break their silence, two elements are needed: trust and safety. These elements are achieved when belonging, a core human need has been established within the environment. When humans have a sense of trust and safety we feel free to present our authentic selves; opening up and sharing who we truly are with those around us.[16]

This commitment to putting down our arms and shields is not for the faint of heart. It demands that we reckon with our limitations, flaws, and fears. It invites us to confront the darkness within and embrace it with love and compassion. In accepting our own brokenness, we find the key to understanding the brokenness of others. Dissolving the patterns that sheath the heart is, at its core, a path to healing and

---

15 Amy Edmondson, *The Fearless Organization: Creating Psychological Safety in the Workplace for Learning, Innovation, and Growth* (Hoboken: Wiley, 2018).

16 Carey Yazeed, "Black Women and Vulnerability: What Brené Brown Got Wrong," April 5, 2023 https://drcareyyazeed.com/2023/04/05/

reconciliation, both within ourselves and in our interactions with the world.

To dissolve the armor that separates us from ourselves and others, we must become both pilgrims and guides, creating a safe haven for exploring our true selves and those of others. We must enlist the courage to listen deeply, witness without judgment, and offer empathy. In these moments of shared vulnerability, we foster genuine connection and solidarity.

To disarm, we must drop the shields of conformity, the masks of perfection, stoicism, and invulnerability. We must shed our gear to protect ourselves from the pain of judgment, ridicule, rejection, and criticism. We must muster up the courage to embrace the paradoxes and ambivalences that arise in our lives.

Shedding our armor is one of the most courageous efforts we can undertake. It requires us to be vulnerable, expose ourselves to the world, and embrace our true selves as we are, with all our imperfections and insecurities. In so doing, we find a way to reciprocate and hold space for others for their vulnerabilities.

In seeing ourselves and allowing ourselves to be seen, we release the armor that has kept us safe but emotionally isolated. Like the Velveteen Rabbit in the children's story, we lose our shiny newness, we lose buttons, but we become real. We find our joyful playfulness again.

Releasing, we pave the way for a life filled with love, belonging, and the richness of authentic relationships. We create a space where the heart can beat freely, unburdened by the weight of shame and fear; we discover the true essence of our humanity and the power of our hearts to love and connect, unencumbered by the armor that once concealed them.

As we dissolve the armor that sheaths the heart, we recognize that strength arises from vulnerability, that wholeness is found in brokenness, and that genuine connection is born out of authenticity. We begin to accept the dual nature of the human experience—the light and the shadow, the joy and the pain, the certainties and the mysteries.

> Sometimes when you're in a dark place you think
> you've been buried, but you've actually been planted.
>
> *Christine Caine*

Heart Questions

1. Were there any unpleasant memories, unacknowledged traumas, or strong emotions that were evoked by reading this chapter?

2. Can you recall a time when you used anger to injure another? A time when anger empowered you to take a stand against some injustice?

3. How has shame manifested in your life? As a moral compass? Or used against you by someone of influence in your life?

Chapter 7

Choosing to Risk Our Values

The human heart is the first home of democracy. It
is where we embrace our questions. Can we be
equitable? Can we be generous? Can we listen
with our whole beings, not just our minds, and
offer our attention rather than our opinions?

Terry Tempest Williams

DURING THE OCCUPATION, Tante Marie, my father's sister, lived in the nearby village of Sliedrecht, which was also occupied by Nazis. When her colleague's Jewish family was called to appear before the Nazis to be processed, Tante Marie intervened. She sheltered the youngest of the children for the entire war.

Tante Marie dyed the girl's hair blond and presented her as a niece whose parents had died in the bombing of Rotterdam. Tante Marie knew she could be betrayed by a neighbor, driven by hunger to collaborate with the Nazis. It happened a lot during the Occupation.

After the war, researchers trying to understand such seemingly extreme altruism conducted interviews with risk-takers like my Tante Marie. A typical response was, "I could do no other."

I have pondered that attitude for years. It's easy to do the right thing when it is safe. How is it that some do it when the cost is high, when it is dangerous? It seems to me that it has something to do with one's sense of self and how we define ourselves and our values. Perhaps it comes from one's sense of belonging and responsibility for others.

My father often said that observing others reveals for whom we genuinely care and are willing to "have skin in the game." Caring deeply isn't always easy. It requires stepping outside our comfort zones and extending our circle of concern beyond the self.

This can be a heavy burden, often unequally distributed. When others don't share the same sense of responsibility, the weight of caring for them can feel unfair and discouraging. It leaves us vulnerable to both physical and emotional exhaustion.

From dialogues with my father, I knew he would say, "I am someone who would not be able to step away when someone else is in danger. Of course I must help. I can do no other." He was in the Resistance; he lived those words. I wonder why he and others I knew could take such risks, sometimes life-threatening to themselves and their families? I never heard that choice framed as a virtue; it was spoken of as something taken for granted. It's just what you do.

Being who he was, he had internalized a moral obligation to help those in need, regardless of the personal cost. However, as a clinical psychologist, I've encountered many with different views. They prioritize self-preservation, setting boundaries, and emphasizing self-care. These sentiments, while understandable, often reflect a culture of affluence and privilege.

Circumstances test our mettle, revealing the strength of our convictions. Some bend like willows in the wind, while others resist and break. My father witnessed both responses among his friends and family. Growing up, thinking of what I would have done if tortured, I often wondered how much pain I could endure before betraying my own values.

Ultimately, the question of how much we're willing to sacrifice for others is profoundly personal. It's a reflection of our individual character and the values we hold dear. But in a world that often celebrates self-interest, it's worth remembering the words of my father: "Giving a damn is hard." It's a challenge, but it also makes us truly human.

Taking risks to help others was an unquestioned assumption that I grew up with. It was validated and echoed by the story of the good Samaritan in the Children's Bible that we read daily. I took it to heart, not as a nice story but as a lesson for how we should treat each other if we were Christians.

Here is the story: Once upon a time, a man walking home was set upon by robbers. They beat him, took his money, and left him by the side of the road. Several different leaders in the village walked by, saw him, and didn't help him. Then, a poor laborer who lived on the wrong side of town saw the poor man. Instead of walking by, he helped him up, took him home, and then went to the authorities to report the robbery. Like other stories in the Children's Bible, I knew that Jesus told this story to teach us that we should always help others, even if they are different.

"For whom will we risk?" often begins with the willingness to risk only for those in our inner circle, our family and close friends. And then, as we mature, we expand and widen our circle of care to include others—first, those who look, think, and believe as we do. If our understanding of interconnection deepens, we widen our circle even more, including those who don't belong or look like us.

And then perhaps to all beings.

What an amazing world that would be!

But we're not there yet. Case in point: in a moment of self-congratulation, most of us have heard someone say, "I love my children so much I would do anything for them. I would even die for them!"

From experience, I know there are people in this world who would do that, not only for their own children but also for the children of others, for children they do not even know.

We all contribute to and are influenced by cultural values, norms, and beliefs about what is and isn't acceptable. It's hard to do the right thing when the risk is significant. Under threats like war or a pandemic, risks grow—and so do the cultural norms for how we respond. This also happened during the Civil Rights movement of the 1960s and the AIDS epidemic, and again after the murder of George Floyd in 2020. In the early months of the second Trump administration, risks are being taken to resist the deportation of immigrants, among many other issues. Risking for the sake of what's right is a never-ending dilemma.

Sometimes, our heart pulls us in one direction while fear or cultural norms and legislated rules pull us in another. We may not like what the mirror reflects back to us. We can cover up the mirror, or we can look more closely.

"I could do no other." Under what circumstance will we say so?

We are continuously challenged and called upon to examine our decisions and actions. "For whom shall I risk?" is a question that arises in big and small ways throughout our day, whether we acknowledge it or not: For whom will we give up our seat on the bus? For whom do we have compassion? For whom do we harbor ill will? In time of great need, for whom will we extend a hand?

TUNING IN TO YOUR VALUES, PASSIONS, AND INMOST REQUEST

The heart is the secret inside the secret.

Rumi

Our values and passions define who we are and influence our choices—how we choose to answer those questions with action, with risk. Understanding these qualities in ourselves is essential for personal growth, self-discovery, and leading a meaningful life.

Values refer to the beliefs and principles that shape our behavior and attitudes. They provide a moral compass and serve as a foundation for our actions. Without reflection, we may not realize what beliefs and principles are underlying our values that lead to our choices. We may act on autopilot instead of with intention. In survival mode, my Tante Marie and my father may not have had the luxury of time to examine their altruism, but their values might be named as honoring human life, responsibility for and love of thy neighbor, even kindness. Values are often instilled in us from our religious or cultural upbringing, and we step into them as if by instinct or years of habit.

But what about the values that lay in the shadows, like not questioning authority or a belief that "might makes right," which can lead to people being harmed or killed? Think of how many atrocities have been committed over time under the guise of aligning with values.

Passions, on the other hand, are the intense interests, enthusiasms, and desires that drive us and bring us joy and fulfillment. Values and passions are interconnected; our values drive our activities, which, in turn, ignite our passions.

Understanding our values and passions allows us to gain deeper insights into our own identity, strengths, and weaknesses. It helps us become more self-aware and in tune with our authentic selves.

When values and passions are aligned, we experience a sense of purpose and fulfillment. We discover a clear direction and motivation to pursue meaningful goals. When they're aligned, they become a compass always pointing to our heart's true north, guiding us toward decisions that matter to us. When we truly understand our values and passions, we can connect with others who share similar beliefs and interests, leading us toward meaningful relationships and communities.

Uncovering your values and passions involves introspection to identify what matters most. First, consider your core beliefs: How would you name your core values? What really matters to you? What brings you joy and fulfillment, and what activities energize you? Notice how you feel when you engage in certain activities or discuss specific topics. This can help you discover new passions, gain a deeper understanding of yourself, and get a glimpse of your heart's inmost request.

For me, the heart's inmost request is like that phrase in the Resistance: "I could do no other." I believe our heart wants to be in alignment with our moral values. It's what makes us feel good at the end of the day, at the end of a party, at the end of meeting with a client, at the end of writing a book, where there's a sense of coherence. How I am in the world is in coherence with who I believe myself to be and want to be.

THE LINK BETWEEN EFFECTIVE
PRESENCE AND SELF-AWARENESS

My love, stay here.
Going in search of Self (as a goal) is illusion;
You are already the One Self.
You will purchase the map,
Only to find you are already Here.

Mooji

One of my core values *and* passions is authentic connection, which requires what I understand as "effective presence." To my mind, effective presence is the capacity to fully inhabit the moment, to be wholeheartedly present to oneself, with others, and within the context in which we find ourselves. Effective presence is inextricably linked to our capacity for self-awareness. That means effective presence and self-awareness are two sides of the same coin, each amplifying the other. Effective presence emerges from the depths of our self-awareness and, in turn, enhances our ability to engage with the world and others in a transformative way.

The practice of self-awareness is where we turn our attention inward toward our thoughts, feelings, motivations, and biases. It's the practice of peeling back the layers of our inner onion to reveal the core of our authentic self. It also involves questions about how we show up in the world, how we impact those around us, and how we, in turn, are influenced by those around us.

My friend Cathy came one day to talk about something troubling her. She felt the delicate balance of self-awareness and effective presence was dwindling in a potluck/book group she hosted. Her friends Don, Susan, Jeffrey, Nancy, George, and John mostly embodied this delicate balance. Don nourished the group with culinary artistry, his awareness attuned to the warmth of shared meals. Susan was also attuned to the physical space and, with quiet grace, helped create a haven of order and cleanliness. Jeffrey, a connoisseur of beauty, elevated the surroundings, his artistic awareness adding a symphony of aesthetics. John's clear thinking and wisdom guided the group when chaos arose. Cathy noted that her own tendencies were in alignment with John's. She too tended to be aware of the need for maintaining order, allowing the group to progress without the obstacles of things undone.

Yet, in this ensemble, there were times when their individual focus was elsewhere, dimming group awareness of the whole. They would partake without mutuality, seemingly oblivious to the unspoken dance of communal effort. George would arrive gaily, seemingly unaware that his shoes had ushered in rain-soaked leaves and mud, or that Cathy would scoop up the leaves before they were distributed. Nancy would talk on and on about an experience she had without awareness that time was limited—that when she was talking, others were listening, or that she was not listening. "When the meetings end," Cathy noted, "some stay to clean up, others leave. I could predict who that would be just as I could predict who would risk providing corrective feedback when it was needed, and whose voice would never be heard."

In my own microcosms of friendship, I've come to understand that awareness is the genesis of service. It is the gentle nudge that awakens us to the needs of others, the subtle alarm that sounds when harmony is disrupted. The value of genuine caring, I've learned, resides in the willingness to be inconvenienced, to shed our metaphorical shoes at the door of another's heart.

Awareness is shaped by culture, the silent conductor guiding our attention. Culture mandates, selects, chooses, cultivates, prioritizes, and otherwise influences awareness. It permeates our individual lives, our neighborhoods, our communities. The invisible hand shapes our relationships, from the grandest to the most intimate.

Awareness—and our values—can also be shaped by adverse childhood experiences, what researchers now shorthand as ACEs.

Perhaps because I was the youngest of eight children in a family constantly beset by survival fears, I had the experience of rarely being truly listened to. This is how life is. In hard times under the pressure of survival, there is little time for attentive listening. For some, not only in times of pressure, it is the norm.

One evening with friends, a woman I'll call Jill shared an experience. She had participated in an active-listening workshop and related how we often listen to our own internal dialogue instead of truly listening to each other's words or minds. She went on to describe how conversations can become mere outpourings of our own thoughts, a preparation for what we want to say next. Instead of engaging with the other person and listening, we tune in to ourselves, ready to launch into our own narrative. Jill spoke of how this hinders the development of intimacy, restricting connection to the level of superficial chitchat.

As Jill spoke, another friend, Mari, jumped in and excitedly informed the group that she was an empath. She then proceeded to do exactly what Jill had been talking about, showing no indication that she had heard Jill's words, but instead pivoting to herself and her own experiences. It was the opposite of active listening. It was a stunning example of "no awareness."

Mari's behavior reminded me of times when I am guilty, times when I have listened to someone talking about sports or auto mechanics or chit-chatting (activities where I have no passion). I may appear to be listening, but I'm not. I'm choosing not to tune in. How often do we do this with each other?

Sometimes it may not matter, because everyone appears to be on the same wavelength and content. At other times, unawareness, not "reading the room" (or each other), can be hurtful and harmful, a deterrent to intimacy. Our capacity varies.

Have you heard of the psychology experiment of the tennis ball painted red on one side, blue on the other side? You show the ball to a group of children of different ages, spinning it to show them that the ball is two colors. You ask them to name what color they see and what color the other children see (who then are positioned to see only one side). Younger children will say, "I see red and they see red." Older children will say, "I see blue and they see red." What this experiment shows is that at a certain age, we humans are not yet able to step into the role of others, not yet able to understand that we see different things from our own perspective.

Just as a certain level of development allows us to understand that not everyone can "role take" (anticipating the reactions and responses of others), not everyone has matured into this level of interpersonal awareness. Nor does everyone have the ability to regulate arising impulses for attention.

We assume that our vision and what we perceive will expand as we grow chronologically older, but it doesn't work that way. Older is not always wiser. We can get stuck in a rut and stay there for years, and sometimes forever.

By contrast, effective presence allows us to be attuned to the unspoken cues of a situation. Whether speaking with a friend, negotiating with a colleague, or in a group situation, effective presence enables us to sense the subtle undercurrents and unspoken needs of those involved. Situational awareness is rooted in a deep connection to our self-awareness, allowing us to read the room while staying true to our values and intentions.

The connection between effective presence and self-awareness is not merely coincidental; it is symbiotic. Effective presence is the outward manifestation of our inner landscape. When we're present to the moment, we are, in fact, present to ourselves, with all our hopes, fears, and vulnerabilities. The quality of our presence reflects the depth of our self-awareness.

This link between effective presence and self-awareness also enhances our relationships. In any human interaction, we're engaging in a dance of presence. Our capacity to be fully present to another person—listening deeply, empathizing, and connecting—is directly correlated to our level of self-awareness.

Cultivating effective presence and self-awareness is a dynamic process that requires conscious cultivation: ongoing reflection, self-inquiry, and practice. This work is often challenged by the cacophony of the external world, which tempts us to disengage from our inner selves and don masks to protect ourselves and create distance between us and the chaos. However, to be present in the most profound sense, we must remain rooted in self-awareness, continually striving to align our inner and outer worlds.

THE LINK BETWEEN SELF-AWARENESS
AND VULNERABILITY

Self-awareness and vulnerability are interdependent qualities. Each requires the other. Each is deepened and enriched by the other. Recognizing and embracing this symbiotic relationship is the key to self-discovery.

Self-awareness (intimacy with self) is the cornerstone of personal growth and authentic living. It's the product of labor, like the blacksmith who hammers hot iron on an anvil to change its shape. It takes energy. Self-awareness is the process of introspection, of turning our gaze inward to confront our true selves. It takes courage to explore our deepest thoughts, feelings, and motivations without judgment or denial. It takes courage to peel back the layers we accumulate through life, seeking the raw, unvarnished truth of who we are. And in this search for self, vulnerability is a powerful tool.

Vulnerability is a portal to our innermost feelings and thoughts, even those we don't want to acknowledge—*especially* those. Be that as it may, when we allow ourselves to experience each feeling as it arises, each emotion as it arises, fully and without judgment, we open ourselves up to the richness of self-awareness: the gift of understanding why we do what we do, and the power to align our thoughts, decisions, and behaviors to our heart's inmost request.

I once had a client I'll call Laura. In our early sessions, her eloquently articulated review about her weekly achievements matched her elegant, polished exterior. As time went on, a masked palpable tension became obvious, her voice laced with a subtle undercurrent of dissatisfaction. I listened, sensing the disconnect between her carefully curated image and the unspoken truths that lived below the surface.

It took a while before Laura dared to reveal herself to me. It came shortly after she had dared to reveal something to herself.

One day, Laura shared a story about a recent work presentation when she had stumbled over her words, her face flushing with embarrassment. But instead of pretending it hadn't happened (and secretly berating herself), she told her audience, "Whoops, I had a moment of audience anxiety there! Let me take a breath or two."

"I still can't believe I could do that," she shared with me. "I would have been mortified in the past," she said. "But now I just accept that I'm human. I was scared, but I could admit it. It's kind of funny. Afterward, several people came up to thank me!"

Tears welled up as she confessed her fear of judgment, her deep-seated belief that she had to be perfect enough to be loved. "I've been so afraid to let people see the real me," she said, her voice thick with emotion. "I thought I had to be perfect to be accepted. But now I realize it's okay to be imperfect and vulnerable. It's actually liberating."

Raw honesty had shown her the way. She had been seen, flaws and all. Her relief was palpable. Laura said quietly, "I'm going to find a way to live like this, to stop being a pretender." (Jackson Browne's song "The Pretender" was popular then.)

From then on, there was a shift and a newfound sense of freedom. Laura no longer had to live up to or under the constraints of some fictional, ego-mandated version of herself. She could consistently embrace her imperfections and speak openly about new aspects of her struggles, fears, and insecurities. Her capacity for authenticity deepened her connections, and she felt a greater ease with herself, which improved her relationships.

In cultures that value strength, control, and invulnerability, it takes courage to relinquish our desire to be seen as flawless, to let down our guard, and share our stories, fears, and struggles. Within these shared experiences, we foster a sense of compassion and empathy for ourselves and others, and by modeling, we invite our communities to do the same. By opening our hearts, we can share the richness and depth of our common human experience—and that's the power of vulnerability.

THE LINK BETWEEN VULNERABILITY AND DEEP CONNECTIONS

Vulnerability is both a path to self-awareness and a bridge to deep connections. When we allow ourselves to be vulnerable, we invite others to do the same. We break down the barriers that separate us and create spaces for genuine human connection. We become more compassionate and empathetic when we have mined the rawness of our own emotions.

In my own life, I have found that the most profound connections I've made were built upon a foundation of vulnerability. When I've allowed myself to be seen—flaws and all—I've witnessed others responding with their own openness. This reciprocity, this shared humanity, has led to relationships that are not merely surface-level interactions but deep, meaningful connections that sustain and nourish the heart's inmost request.

Deep connections require an honest and unguarded exchange—in places and with people you can trust. (With self-awareness and reflection, you learn to trust your inner discernment about whom you can trust and when you can stretch yourself to open your heart.) Deep connections flourish when we allow our authentic selves to emerge, unfiltered and unapologetic. By opening ourselves to the possibility of being hurt or misunderstood, we create an environment where genuine connection can take root, where pretense and superficiality have no place, and where the raw, unvarnished truth of our existence can be recognized and celebrated.

Deep connections provide us with a sense of empowerment, which is not just about what we receive but what we give. We are empowered when we make the shift from the small me to the big WE. This shift is where we find solace, support, and the knowledge that we are not alone in our struggles.

Deep connections are more than a source of comfort and support; they are a wellspring of creativity and growth. When we engage in meaningful dialogues and exchanges with others, our minds and hearts are opened to new perspectives and ideas. We challenge our assumptions and broaden our horizons. In the moments of deep connection, we discover new insights and possibilities, forging a path toward both personal and collective growth.

A caveat is that it is all too easy to let the moments of connection pass us by unnoticed. Often, it's in the pause between breaths, the quiet spaces between words, moments when we're fully present, when we truly listen to one another—in these times we experience the deepest and most profound connections.

When we're brave enough, and steadfast enough, to offer the world our unwavering presence, we are creating what Jean Oelwang, author of *Partnering*, calls "magnetic moments." According to Oelwang, magnetic moments are "intentional experiences that allow for people to be present together," whether rituals, traditions, or daily practices.[17]

Magnetic moments can also be deeply transformative with the power to bring greater meaning, joy, and understanding into our lives—for being *deeply connected* is an intrinsic quality of our existence, one that tells us who we are.

> Creating [magnetic moments] takes thought,
> planning, and effort, but they are worth it
> because of the way they increase the depth
> and meaning of the connections you form.
>
> *Jean Oelwang*

MEE LEEVEN: VALUING EACH OTHER

The heart has a remarkable capacity to break open during the darkest of times and in moments of great peril. The very idea of a breaking heart often conjures images of fragility and vulnerability—and yet, as Leonard Cohen lyrically tells us, the cracks in our heart let the light in. In the darkest of nights, the heart can reveal extraordinary connection and unequaled depth of humanity. I recognize the truth of this from my own history.

Despite my first years unfolding in the chaos and brutality of WWII, the suffering took place amid the most beautiful aspects of humanity. There were those whose hearts transcended the boundaries of self-interest. Who risked life and limb and all that was precious. Men and women who risked, willing to pay the cost of personal danger, even torture and

---

17 Jean Oelwang. *Partnering: Forge the Deep Connections That Make Things Happen* (New York: Optimism Press, 2022).

the loss of life itself, who felt that they "could do no other" but come to the aid of strangers hunted by the Nazis. These hearts could not abandon others to harm. They resisted and stood in the way.

Women like my aunt harboring the Jewish girl. And men like my father and a young soldier he met one night.

Dad was a contractor, a dike-builder. That meant my father knew every inlet and outlet in the village like the back of his hand. He also knew the *biesbos*—those watery, reeded lowlands adjacent to the town that gave access to the North Sea. That knowledge made him strategically crucial to the Resistance.

The biesbos provided hiding places and escape routes for those fleeing capture, including downed British pilots, men fleeing Nazi labor camps, and others the Germans deemed "undesirable." The Resistance guided them through the biesbos to waiting boats at low tide. When the tides rose, they headed for open waterways, where they met larger boats destined for the North Sea and then the English Channel.

My father also knew the farmers, some of whom still had potatoes and turnips long after none remained in our village. One evening, under the cover of darkness, he broke curfew by setting out in a small boat, hoping against hope to bring back food for the family. Breaking curfew was punishable by death. But we were starving, so he went.

Hours later, after scoring a small bag of potatoes, he guided the boat back up the river that opened into a stream behind our home—where a young German soldier on night patrol stopped him.

Soldier and father stood frozen, staring at each other, eyes wide, surprised, and filled with fear. Moments passed, thick with tension. Then, slowly, cautiously, my father pulled back the burlap sack to reveal the potatoes. "I have a wife and eight children," he said solemnly.

The young soldier's gaze moved from my father to the potatoes, then back to my father. He paused, hesitating. Then, he slowly lowered his weapon, turned, and walked away.

My father shared with me what happened that night only years later, when I was old enough to appreciate the humanity this story revealed. He told the tale quietly. He didn't hold back. He admitted, in no uncertain terms, that at that moment, his life and the lives of our entire family were on the line. Stressing also that at that moment, the young German soldier put his own life on the line for insubordination.

Telling this story, my father knew it was a teaching moment, an opportunity to remind me of the values he lived by. He frequently summed up values in a four familiar words from the village dialect: *we moeten mee leeven*, which roughly translates to "we must live together and for each other."

Remembering this story and reliving it as I write these words, I am overcome with gratitude and awe—the courage it must have taken when the price of failure was so high.

WHERE FEAR AND LOVE MEET

There's really no way of judging where kindness begins and where it ends. The kindness shown to my father by the young soldier on that fateful night will live on forever in the hearts and minds of our family and those who shared in the bounty that day. A kindness that continues to echo through time and space as it touches the hearts of those reading these lines and stretches into the future as the story is retold.

It is a story about remaining human in the face of fear. Ultimately, it's a story about human nature that has taken many shapes throughout our brief history.

Not all Dutch people were "good," and not all German soldiers were "bad." Good and evil reside in all of us. As does courage and cowardice, self-awareness and self-deception. Danger brings out the best and the worst in us. Often, the brave find their cowardice exposed; the cowards, their bravery.

Throughout the war, the skies overhead were busy with bombers from both sides: some were German planes bound for London, some were British planes bound for Germany. Antiaircraft guns mounted on our village grounds brought many of the British planes down. Young British pilots, aircraft, and bombs frequently fell on our village.

When the defeat of Germany was imminent, the same British bomber pilots who once dropped bombs now volunteered to drop boxes of food to the starving people of our village. It was a dangerous humanitarian mission. British planes had to fly perilously low to make the drops. Although defeat was imminent, German antiaircraft guns were still mounted, loaded, and manned.

Even so, not a single British plane was shot down.

No one is always right; no one is always wrong. It is rarely black or white. The British soldiers took a significant risk. The German soldiers manning the antiaircraft guns also took a considerable risk—refusing to shoot down those British planes was punishable by death. It was time to rest and lay down their arms. A time when fear and love meet—and the heart breaks open.

The heart's capacity to value forgiveness and reconciliation can be astonishing. Despite the overwhelming bitterness and hatred that conflict can breed, individuals who have endured the most profound hardships often find it within themselves to extend forgiveness. They do so not to condone the atrocities but to break the cycle of violence and heal the wounds that war inflicts. In these moments, the heart's resilience shines through, proving that even in the darkest hours, it can foster a vision of hope and transformation.

> Life is short. We don't have much time to gladden
> the hearts of those who walk this way with us.
> So, be swift to love and make haste to be kind.

Henri-Frédéric Amiel

Heart Questions

1. List the values and passions that define who you are. Which of your values are your own, and which did you inherit from your family or culture?

2. How do these values and passions influence the choices you make?

3. Looking back at your life, can you identify a time when self-awareness and vulnerability showed up in a surprising way? How did you respond?

Chapter 8

Keeping Your Heart Open in Uncertain Times

To be hopeful in bad times is not just foolishly romantic. It is based on the fact that human history is a history not only of cruelty, but also of compassion, sacrifice, courage, kindness.

Howard Zinn

———

I WAS TOO young to remember much about the Occupation, so I called my last remaining sibling, who is in her nineties now. "Food was scarce," Nelly said, "and then scarcer. Nazis moved into our grandparents' home. Children weren't allowed in the fields because of landmines. Blackout curtains were hung over windows so Allied bombers couldn't use our lights for navigation during night raids on German cities. Failure to comply could mean death."

Nelly was 11 years old when I was born. She was my primary caretaker, more of a mother to me than a sister. "When you were a babe, we would throw you in a tub and run for shelter when the sirens wailed. When you got too big for the tub, you slept next to Dad so he could scoop you up and run. Sometimes, the shelter was a barn. Sometimes, a riverboat."

"At times," Nelly said, "I still hear the wail of those sirens."

After a long pause, she continued, "I feel the fear deep in my gut. I smell the smoke we inhaled as we ran for shelter. These things are just a part of me." Nelly was reluctant to talk about it. It was painful for her to dig up these old memories, but when I told her I was writing a book including the story of our life in the war, she wanted to contribute.

And she did contribute—until her nightmares returned.

I was too young to experience the kind of fear that Nelly felt, but it was in the air we breathed so I must have picked up on it, sensed it in others. Also, my youthful innocence was protected by my family. Perhaps for them, my playfulness offered moments of reprieve, even glimpses of normalcy. So, while I must have sensed it, I did not experience fear as a personal threat. It existed for others who were taking care of me. I felt protected in its presence.

My family, however, felt a different kind of fear. They lived in a different reality. They understood what I didn't: that no one is safe in war. For them, fear was very personal; its all-pervading presence marked every waking moment for five insufferable years.

As I started to write this book eight decades after the war, sitting at my dining table in a suburb of Minneapolis, gazing out the window at my beloved neighborhood of many years, I felt sad. The street in front of my house—once boisterous and vibrant, with children laughing and playing, with neighbors stopping to admire the gardens—was silent.

It had been months since COVID invaded our communities, isolating people in their homes, fear spreading faster than the virus. Schools, shops, theatres, and even parks were closed.

My friends and neighbors worried about their jobs and mortgages. I saw images on TV of entire families waiting in food lines for their rations, hoping it would be enough. All of us wondering how long the pandemic would last, hoping to outlive it.

A friend called to talk about his children's education. Would schools reopen? And if they did, would the kids be behind? Would they be safe? His anxious uncertainty was palpable.

I wondered if his questions could be answered by my own family's hindsight. I was only four when the war ended, too young for school, so I reached for my phone to call Nelly.

"At first, classes were limited," she told me. "Then they became sporadic, and finally, education ended entirely as hunger and exhaustion overwhelmed the village. There were worse things than lost education."

I knew where her mind was going. The Resistance saved hundreds from forced labor camps or worse. The crawl space under our floor was sometimes occupied, the opening covered with a rug and a small table.

"Luckily," Nelly said, "we never got raided."

Unlike the Occupation, when I was too young and protected to understand, as I wrote these words, staring out at the deserted street, I, too, felt the pain—the coil of fear in my gut, the loneliness.

CHOOSING TO GROW OUR HEART

In any given moment we have two options: to step forward into growth or to step back into safety.

Abraham Maslow

Studies show that the highest potential for personal growth may follow experiences that shake us to our core. Post-traumatic growth is a new term used to describe this opportunity. Difficult times can force us to make choices and reevaluate our most strongly held beliefs about who we are, what we believe is right, and what our responsibility is.

Hard times provide possibilities, and practice makes them possible. When life becomes uncertain and uncontrollable, we learn patience and acceptance. When we feel raw, exposed, and vulnerable, we learn compassion. When we're forced to turn to others, we learn to connect. When we've exhausted every avenue, we turn inward and discover a well of untapped inner strength. Sometimes, adversity makes us stronger, more resilient, and more authentic. Sometimes, it gives birth to hidden aspects of who we are, to qualities that are until then unrealized. We may not notice our heart is growing until much later.

DUTCH HUNGER WINTER

One of my earliest childhood memories happened in the winter of 1944. It was called Dutch Hunger Winter, and the lasting effects of that winter are still being studied by epigenetic scientists today.

It was the last year of the war. The Germans knew the war was over. Some parts of the Netherlands were already liberated by the Canadians. Even though they had nothing to gain—seemingly driven by malice alone, or perhaps retaliation for the Resistance blowing up a bridge to their supply lines—they set up blockades to prevent food or supplies from reaching some parts of the province of South Holland, including my village.

Food was nonexistent, except for the meager rations doled out at the soup kitchen, now reduced to 400 calories a day. Neighbors were succumbing to starvation, and we teetered on the brink ourselves.

balance in the system. And I wanted to be brave, like those in the Resistance.

This self-realization came to me when one of my teenage clients complained about how her parents were always concerned about what the neighbors might think. She concluded, "F*ck it, let's give them something exciting then." And then she leaned to dramatic means to act out.

My response to fear was, *I can show you. I can do hard things. I can hitchhike, and I can go to the Hindu Kush. I can dive with sharks and seek complexity where you seek simplicity.* I wanted to dance with fear, not avoid it. Because I grew up in Canada in a different time, I didn't value safety as much as my parents did.

Despite (or perhaps because of) early years of childhood at war, marked with chaos, poverty, and uncertainty, I have chosen to travel the world, often alone, as an adventurer, not a five-star-hotel tourist. In so doing, I have had unforgettable experiences of meeting and getting to know fascinating people. It has allowed me to live my dreams: to stand on the cliffs of the Karakoram and the Hindu Kush mountains, dive into caves in the ocean's depths, and do relief work in Sri Lanka after the tsunami.

Fear was not absent on those journeys. It traveled with me. More than once terror has clinched my gut. Somehow, by some grace, I was able to let it pass, to go forward. More than once, I've made heartfelt promises to God, "If you get me through this one, I'll never do this again." Then I shrugged it off the next day.

I am grateful for all of it, including the terror in my gut.

Even so, there are times when my ability to overcome fear fails me. The wailing of a bomb siren in an old movie can freeze me in my seat. *The Empire of the Sun* left me with flashbacks for days. I once watched a film in which a group of German and Dutchmen conversed in both languages and had flashbacks for a week.

For these moments, too, I am grateful.

TRAUMA AND TRIGGER WARNINGS

I must admit, the warnings on television or online that tell us that material may be traumatizing freak me out. The perceived and assumed vulnerability freaks me out.

As a psychologist, I have worked with victims of torture. With war survivors, women who have been raped, gang raped, and individuals who have been brutally sexually abused in the family. The television warnings and the quick-to-be traumatized responses of individuals who need years of somatic therapy to heal are paradoxical and strange to me. Why is it that some people survive terrible wounds and end up happy, helpful, productive, and achieving, while others are laid low?

There's a Dutch cultural part to my disdain for fragility. The Dutch don't take well to fragility or trauma drama. Additionally, my travel experiences have taken me to places where life is harsh, and the comforts that are part of our privileged lives are unknown. Thus, I may see through a different lens. My own life experiences, my familiarity with the "third world," as well as the experiences of people I have met in my office, taught me that few of us escape physical wounds: stubbing our toes, broken fingers, being hit, burned, and more serious ones like major infections and broken bones, big-bone surgeries.

Even the most fortunate among us also typically sustain some form of psychological wounds—"heart wounds" such as neglect, abuse, violence, unfair treatment, cruelty, being overlooked, shunned, being expected to do things that we're not capable of, judged, blamed, not seen, and exposed to violence. We witness cruelty to others. Many of us experience loss of innocence and meet existential questions prematurely. Beyond our individual capacities, we are limited—or supported—by structural influences.

Exploring the human capacity to overcome potentially harmful experiences with resilience has been a focus of research for my friend, child psychologist Ann Masten, author of *Ordinary Magic*. Masten is a Distinguished McKnight University Professor in the Institute of Child Development at the University of Minnesota. She is internationally known for her research on competence, risk, and multisystem resilience in human development. "Families, schools, communities, cultures, and governments all play vital roles in the development of resilience in their children, who in turn protect the future resilience of societies," Masten asserts.[18]

One of the questions she says we need to address in today's complex world is this:

"Given the biological wear and tear that can arise within individuals in contexts of structural racism or discrimination, marginalization, and oppression (even among high achieving individuals), how can schools, communities, and/ or states confront and dismantle structural and deeply embedded forms of racism, injustice, trauma, or persecution that can pose lifelong threats to healthy development and well-being?"

While confronting those challenges may sound daunting, Masten finds hope. By studying how to prevent or mitigate exposure to adversity, boosting resources, and

---

18 Ann S. Masten, "Emergence and Evolution of Developmental Resilience Science over Half a Century," Development and Psychopathology 36, no. 5 (2024): 2542–2550, https://doi.org/10.1017/S0954579424000154.

building protections, we can understand how to nurture our human capacity to survive, learn, and even flourish— "on small and large scales, spanning challenges from the cellular to global level, and momentary to evolutionary time scales."[19]

THE THREE CIRCLES OF ACTION

For those of us who grow up with the privileges of safety and "helicopter care," wounds can begin to call our princess-like expectations into question. Wounds can set us on a path of meeting life as it is, as not just joy and safety but also suffering.

The Buddha teaches that suffering is part of life simply because we humans are prone to attachment, desire, and delusion. However, we can also overcome these states of mind-heart through our choices and actions.

Pema Chödrön offers a compelling pathway beyond suffering. She describes three concentric circles where the inner ring represents the comfortable and familiar, the second circle represents learning, and the outer ring, excessive risk. These zones represent different states of mind and choices we make.[20]

The comfort zone is where we feel safe and in control. It's where we rely on well-worn habits and patterns, seeking predictability. But if you stay here too long, it shrinks. The challenge zone is the realm of learning and growth. It's

---

19 Masten, "Emergence and Evolution."

20 Pema Chödrön. *Welcoming the Unwelcome: Wholehearted Living in a Brokenhearted World*. Boulder: Shambhala, 2019.

where we venture beyond our familiar routines, facing our fears and embracing new possibilities. The outer circle, the zone of excessive risk, is where we endanger or re-traumatize ourselves, like diving into the deep end without knowing how to swim.

Chödrön encourages us to move beyond the comfort zone and into the challenge zone, not recklessly or with disregard for danger, but with mindful intention. This is where growth happens. I imagine yet another zone I call the realization zone, a place of awakening and transformation. It's where we discover our true potential and experience a deeper connection to ourselves and the world..

Chödrön's three circles of action are potent tools for self-reflection and personal growth. We all navigate this spectrum. We learn through trial and error to make conscious choices that will allow us to make meaningful contributions to the world.

In my own family, my parents' choice to leave Holland after the war was a pivotal time of risking change and leaving our comfort zone..

FROM RECONSTRUCTION TO RELOCATION

By May of 1945, Holland was free again, but large swaths of countryside, villages, towns, and cities had been destroyed. Our small village tried to assemble itself amid so many broken pieces. When the Nazis left, we had to deal with what had happened. Reconnecting under such widespread devastation, emotional exhaustion, and betrayal proved a steep hurdle.

During the war, some in our village betrayed those in the Resistance—sometimes to appease the occupying forces, sometimes in exchange for extra food tokens. Dutch men were scarce during the five years of occupation. With many men at war or hiding, some young women had fallen in love with German soldiers billeted in the village. After the war, choices were underlined and highlighted. All were brought to account for their choices.

People knew who had collaborated. It became a branding. They never lost that identity even 40 years later; my father still referred to someone as "Jan, the Nazi sympathizer" or 'Piet the betrayer." Some stayed in the village, some moved away—perhaps even changed their names, hoping to escape their reputation.

My father was selected and appointed by *den Haag*, the Netherlands' equivalent to Washington, DC, to reconstitute the village. That meant identifying Nazi sympathizers and bringing them to justice. It meant revitalizing businesses. It meant holding people accountable for things done, and things failed to do.

The village justice courts were public places. Reconstruction takes time. The dead were mourned. Justice was restored. Rubble was cleared, and new pathways for food and ways to heat the house were found. People reconnected with family and friends.

The post-war Dutch economy was zero; Stalin loomed in the East, the war in Indonesia had started, and Dutch men were again being conscripted. The Dutch government promoted emigration to Australia, Brazil, and Canada. With Europe in shambles, the future held no promise or security.

Before the Occupation, my father was a businessman. During the war, his business—along with thousands of others—was wiped out. No one could see how the social structure would be rebuilt. With socialism on the rise, my father saw no future for his sons. My brother Basil, the oldest son in our patriarchal family, became a draft dodger to flee the War of Independence in Indonesia, a Dutch colony from 1605 to 1949. He found a sponsor in Canada in 1948 and became indentured to avoid going to another war. Indenture was a way poor people could travel in exchange for work as servants or apprentices. It was sometimes fair, but sometimes people were treated badly. The sponsor agreed to take us in return for the indenture of my brother and one of my sisters. The entire family followed in 1949, a year later.

LIMINAL SPACES: PORTALS TO BECOMING

In the universe, there are things that are
known, and things that are unknown, and
in between them, there are doors.

William Blake

I don't remember much about leaving Holland, but I think for my family it must have been a time of uncertainty, ambivalence, and ambiguity—the very meaning of "liminal." My father was in his mid-fifties, with a wife and eight kids, and none of us spoke English. We left Holland penniless. As I mentioned previously, post-war reconstruction didn't allow emigrants to take money out of the country. What money and assets remained after the war were left with family. I asked Nelly about this time, but she really didn't want to go there. It's too painful. I understand.

When we boarded the *Volendam* in July 1949, we could only bring two boxes and a bicycle. The journey across the Atlantic took ten days. One of the things I remember was the food, always available on a buffet. I had never seen food like that, food you could eat anytime you wanted to. The ocean was rough. It seemed everyone got seasick except me. I roamed the decks while everyone else was throwing up over the railings. I saw flying fish! I felt very resilient and excited, sleeping in the hold with people all around me. That was just fine with me, but my mother was horrified. She was very private. She never stopped vomiting from the seasickness until the ship came down the St. Lawrence River, landing in Quebec. I turned eight years old a week later.

As a child, I had no comprehension of what it would mean in my life to leave Holland—no inner understanding that when I stepped onto the deck of the *Volendam*, I would be leaving not only the land my ancestors had lived on for unknown generations but my shared personal and familial history, my earliest friends, four grandparents, thirty-nine uncles and aunts, and my mother tongue. In my later years, now, I feel the legacy of uprootedness.

The *Volendam*, a refurbished troop carrier, took us into a liminal, watery zone between the known and the unknown, an in-between place where one thing ends and the next is yet to come.

As it turned out, it was an initiation. I would return to liminal space many times throughout my life.

LIMINAL ZONES ARE HEART SPACES

Embracing the in-between space is about pushing beyond the boundaries of our comfort zone. It's about venturing into the ambiguous, the transitional, the place of uncertainty. And for human beings, uncertainty is scary as hell. We go to great lengths to avoid it. But for those with courageous hearts, it's also a place of promise, where personal growth, creativity, and a deeper understanding of ourselves and the world around us await on the other side.

In the liminal, we know that we don't know, that we can't even pretend to know. In the liminal, none of our masks fit anymore. We don't have the answers. We don't even know the questions. We're forced to adapt, learn something new, and open our hearts and minds to this uncharted territory. The only currency that matters here is vigilance, acceptance, the ability to let go, and resilience.

The liminal is a space of potential transformation. It challenges us to adapt, learn, and evolve. It's where creative breakthroughs can happen as we open ourselves to new ideas, perspectives, and insights. It's where we can view the world from different lenses and different angles. It's a time of questioning, seeking meaning, and connecting with a higher purpose or a deeper sense of self.

By exploring the liminal space, we can learn to make more informed and thoughtful decisions, weigh our options, consider consequences, and choose paths that align with our values and aspirations. It's about becoming more adaptable and less fearful.

The tricky part is recognizing the liminal when you're in it and figuring out how to move through it rather than getting stuck there. Liminal spaces are places of risk and opportunity. They are portals to becoming, meaning that opportunity awaits you on the other side. The risk is staying so long in the void that it becomes a destination rather than a door.

LIMINAL STATES OF FEAR AND OPPORTUNITY

Not all liminal spaces I've encountered are as dramatic as my eight-year-old transatlantic journey aboard the *Volendam*. There have been times when I walked right into the liminal with my eyes wide open.

I was in my forties when I followed my heart's desire to be a diver. I had just finished my PhD, and I was encouraged to dive by my friend Kevin, an avid, experienced diver and psychiatrist who convinced me that I could do it. I had had lung problems in my childhood, and my pulmonologist, whom I was required to see to pass the diving certification, said my lungs were okay but suggested that diving wasn't altogether a good idea.

I did it anyway. I did not yet know how to swim, only to dog paddle, but I learned to swim so that I could pass the diving course. I learned how to "free dive" to the bottom of the swimming pool and pick up objects. I learned how to swim the required distance to meet the qualifications. From then on, I swam a mile a day most days to keep myself in shape and ready to dive when the opportunity came.

I met most of my certification requirements in Minnesota. My check-out dive for certification was in the Red Sea, where I had met a friend in Hurghada on the Egyptian coast. The day of the test, I sat on the boat deck, terrified.

As luck would have it, the dive master must have seen the symptoms. Knowing I was there to be certified, he closely watched me as I descended. By the time I was 40 feet deep, I knew I was in trouble. My Egyptian equipment was falling off, no longer supported by the shoulder strap that had been rotted away by time and exposure to the sea. But I lucked out. He saw and quietly swam toward me, hand signaling, making eye contact. "Okay?"

"Yes!"

He signaled to breathe naturally. We were going up! I nodded and relaxed, and he guided me slowly to the surface.

After my PADI certification dive in the Red Sea, and multiple excursions in Mexico, the Caymans, Belize, and Honduras, a dive master friend assured me I was ready to dive Cocos Island, a wild ocean site where hammerheads schooled, manta rays were as big as a car, and whale sharks could often be seen.

When the dive master, a retired Navy Seal named Jerry, first encouraged me to come on the Cocos trip, I was hesitant. With less than a hundred dives under my belt, I asked, "Are you sure I'm ready?"

We had been on trips together before. He shrugged, "Sure. Why not?"

It was settled then. I would come.

I flew to Costa Rica and boarded the *Okeanos*, a yacht where I would live and dive for the next 10 days.

When the *Okeanos* headed for the open waters of the Pacific Ocean, it seemed like a dream. My mind was filled with visions of swimming with orcas and large pelagic fish such as swordfish, marlin, and bluefin tuna—but most of all, I dreamed of swimming alongside a whale shark!

This would be a grand adventure, the adventure of a lifetime!

It was—but not in the way I imagined.

We were only a few miles out when I learned that I was far and away the team rookie. That would have been alarming enough. But I couldn't find a dive buddy before I signed on. I came alone. Luckily, there was one other solo diver, so we were assigned to each other.

As night fell the first evening, we all settled our scuba gear on the deck, checking our equipment and getting ready for the first dive. My heart pounded against my chest. I did my best to be blasé. But in truth, I was terrified.

It turned out most of the divers were dive masters. Everyone was very excited and seemingly unconcerned. They took turns telling stories of previous adventures, illuminating in detail how a diver could quickly find themselves in a life-threatening situation. They laughed or applauded or shook their heads in awe. Before long, the conversation turned to what everyone hoped would be the most incredible thrill: a chance to swim with a whale shark.

At dinner, our guides set down the rules for tomorrow's dive. Most notable was the ominous disclaimer, a warning: "We will take the zodiac to the dive site. The waves are high, and the underwater currents are strong. You are on your own down there. If you get lost, we cannot save you. We'll do what we can, but the waves are too high and choppy to see you in the water. A current can quickly take you out beyond the range of vision. Dive at your own risk."

I had planned to be afraid of sharks, but not this!

That evening, I climbed into my small berth with a stomach full of knots. The voice inside my head accused me of overshooting my better judgment. As I lay there, tossing and turning, I weighed my options: I could say I was sick or that I hadn't slept well, so it was unsafe for me to dive. Or I could confess that I made a mistake when signing up.

At some point, I finally fell asleep.

I woke suddenly to the screeching voice of a parrot. I rubbed my eyes and squinted toward the sound. A green parrot swayed atop my perch's swinging louver door, head bobbing. He stared at me arrogantly, then puffed out his chest and screeched again. "Time to dive. Time to dive," he announced with great authority. Assuming, I imagine, that he'd fulfilled his duty, he turned away. I didn't move. My body refused. Walls of fear closed in as waves of panic surged through me.

The feathered little pest turned back; his piercing black eyes peered into mine. Then he did the most remarkable thing: he tilted his head and, quite seductively, offered what sounded like a promise, "Whale shark, whale shark," he screeched.

The effect was magical.

A surge of excitement washed through the fear, pushing back the walls and creating the space for both the promise of adventure—*and* the fear of it. I felt my body release and open up. The fear was still there, but now there was enough space to allow movement. A renewed sense of excitement poured in.

Fear wasn't diminished, not at all. But it was diluted. It no longer owned me. A type of harmony arose as I held the tension between these two powerful emotions—without trying to escape them.

When the energies of fear and excitement synchronize, something unique happens. They begin to speak to each other, to inform each other. And that's a good thing: too much excitement throws caution to the wind while too much fear freezes you up.

From the interplay of fear and excitement, freedom arose. Not freedom from fear, but freedom within it—right there in the center of it. My pounding heart settled into this place where promise and fear meet, where risk coexists with opportunity and a choice is required.

"Time to dive. Time to dive," came the screech from the louver door.

The knots in my stomach were released.

I reached for my gear.

> The only thing that makes life possible is permanent, intolerable uncertainty: not knowing what comes next.
>
> *Ursula K. Le Guin*

Heart Questions

When life becomes uncertain and uncontrollable,
we learn patience and acceptance. When we feel raw,
exposed, and vulnerable, we learn compassion.
When we're forced to turn to others, we learn to
connect. When we've exhausted every avenue, we
turn inward and discover a well of untapped
inner strength.

1. Referring to this paragraph from the current chapter, recall times in your life when:
   a. Your life became uncertain and uncontrollable.
   b. You felt raw, exposed, and vulnerable.
   c. You were forced to turn to others for help.
   d. You were forced to turn inward and rely only on your inner strength.

2. If you reframed those times as liminal portals of growth, how would you rewrite those narratives?

Chapter 9

Reclaiming Happiness and Belonging, Resisting Toxic Positivity

Now and then it's good to pause in our
pursuit of happiness and just be happy.

Guillaume Apollinaire

———

WISDOM TEACHERS FROM around the world tell us that human beings' primary goal is happiness. However, as His Holiness the Dalai Lama has pointed out, we don't want to suffer, but we run toward it. We seek happiness, but we often turn our backs on it.

The Venerable Matthieu Ricard, a scientist and a Tibetan Buddhist monk, has reluctantly been called the "happiest man in the world." Ricard participated in a 12-year brain study on meditation and compassion at the University of Wisconsin. While regions of his brain lit up (and countless other research has repeated the results since then), happiness is both science of the mind and a choice of the human heart.

For Ricard, happiness comes from an ongoing practice to be aware of your thoughts, to clarify your emotions, and to choose your reactions to any given experience. While talking to Krista Tippett during an *On Being* interview, Ricard talked of consciously choosing humor in a challenging situation. He gave the example of how, during project visits to schools and clinics in Tibet, the team's car can often get stuck in the middle of a river. "A big stream, it's raining . . . you can imagine some people screaming, upset. Usually, it ends up everyone is on top of the car, cracking into laughter. Such—they think it's such a funny thing. [laughs] . . . we do our best, and things happen, and why should you take it too seriously, because we will survive that, hopefully, and after all, what's the problem? It's just one part of the journey, and it's so much more fun if you take it like that than making all these tantrums about things."[21]

A significant contributor to all the confusion about happiness is that happiness is complex. There are different kinds of happiness. Some happiness is self-focused, simple, material, and short-lived. A greater, deeper form of happiness demands more of us: a purpose that is bigger than ourselves, meaningful relationships, social engagement, personal growth, and self-acceptance. Philosophers and spiritual leaders have stressed the differences for centuries, yet the confusion persists.

THE EXHAUSTION OF CHASING HAPPINESS

Hedonic happiness is a common form of happiness. It's the happiness you feel when you get something you want—a new car, a pay raise, a trip to Hawaii, or maybe just a good meal at your favorite restaurant. It depends on what's going on "out there."

Hedonic happiness is about getting what we want, when and how we want it. Or what Matthieu Ricard referred to in

---

21 Matthieu Ricard, interview by Krista Tippett, "Matthieu Ricard: Happiness as Human Flourishing," *On Being with Krista Tippett*, podcast November 12, 2009, MP3 audio, 92:41, https://onbeing.org/programs/matthieu-ricard-happiness-as-human-flourishing-jul2017/.

his *On Being* interview as "an endless succession of pleasurable experiences," which, on the surface, sounds pretty good, right? He called it a "recipe for exhaustion."

Hedonic pleasure is entirely dependent upon time and outer circumstances. But time and circumstances are constantly changing. Seeking after pleasure, thinking about how to make things better for ourselves all the time, can be exhausting and stressful. Ultimately, it leads only to an empty unhappiness.

We know this. Pleasure even exhausts itself out! For example, dessert after a good meal is lovely. But two desserts? Not so much. You buy a new car, and looking at it makes you smile, but by the time the first payment rolls in—not so much. The object you so craved is still parked in your garage, but the pleasure has been used up.

Hedonic happiness often finds us chasing after the next new thing. A pursuit that leaves you happy one moment, ambivalent and even despairing the next. We may settle for hedonic happiness because we think it's the best we can hope for. Unfortunately, it has a short and limited lifespan.

SEEKING ABIDING HAPPINESS

Eudaimonic happiness, on the other hand, does not depend on external events. Eudaimonic happiness is an abiding happiness. It does not break down under modern life's high-paced, over-stretched schedules. It may even protect us against the pressures of overstretched schedules that arise as we chase one shiny object after another. Eudemonic happiness has to do with finding our purpose and meaning in life, which is a natural extension of discerning our values and passions, our heart's deepest desires.

Fortunately, eudaimonic happiness does not exclude the pleasurable moments of hedonic happiness—nor do they limit it. So, these two kinds of happiness do not oppose each other. Like all seeming opposites, hedonic and eudaimonic happiness exist on a spectrum: they can, and often do, overlap each other.

The difference between hedonic and eudaimonic happiness is not a new idea. However, what is new is the recent discovery of how these two types of happiness affect us on a molecular level.

Barbara L. Fredrickson of the University of North Carolina and her team looked at the biological influence of hedonic and eudaimonic happiness. They wanted to know if the two kinds of happiness affect us on the level of our genes. It turns out that they do.

While both offer a feeling of satisfaction, hedonic and eudaimonic happiness are experienced very differently within our immune cells. Hedonic pleasures are associated with an increased expression of the genes involved in inflammation, which could explain the rise in inflammatory diseases such as arthritis and heart disease. Eudaimonic pleasures are associated with decreased expression of those same genes. Here's Dr. Fredrickson in her own words:

> We can make ourselves happy through simple pleasures, but those "empty calories" don't help us broaden our awareness or build our capacity in ways that benefit us physically. At the cellular level, our bodies appear to respond better to a different kind of well-being, one based on a sense of connectedness and purpose.[22]

---

22 University of North Carolina at Chapel Hill. "Human cells respond in healthy, unhealthy ways to different kinds of happiness." ScienceDaily. www.sciencedaily.com/releases/2013/07/130729161952.htm

IS HAPPINESS LINKED TO A SENSE OF BELONGING?

Is it possible to be happy even in the worst of circumstances, or in a life full of challenge and heartache? If it were not, how could we survive much less thrive in this world?

On the day we stepped onto the *Volendam*, the converted troop ship that would take us across the Atlantic, my family and I lost our large extended family, childhood culture, language, and national identity. Although I have visited Holland briefly at times, I have lived away from my homeland for most of my life. Perhaps that's why I've spent most of my life exploring the sense of belonging, purpose, and connectedness. I've always been driven by a knowing in my heart, an awareness of something more profound than life on the surface, by something that *feels* cellular.

Since leaving Holland, I've been a resident of four countries and a citizen of three. I've also owned a tiny stone cottage on Gökçeada, an island in the Dardanelles. Despite the distance, my native culture, language, family, and birth country remain a source of identity and pride, a way of remaining connected to my roots and the ancestors I once knew briefly but was cut off from—and miss.

My father often called me "Benjamin" after the youngest son of Jacob. Perhaps that is why I sometimes think of the story "Joseph, Son of Jacob," a beloved tale found in the Old Testament of the Children's Bible that we read at the end of meals. Like Joseph and millions of others, I have skipped across class boundaries and religious traditions. Today, I still claim my native language but have no country that truly feels like home. In its place, I have shaped and reshaped my sense of identity. My heart's sense of belonging is dispersed between Holland, Canada (where my family of origin still lives), the United States, and other countries where I have found "connections." I have learned to think of myself as a citizen of the world and to consider the planet as home.

But a sense of a personal home eludes me. I belong everywhere and nowhere. In some ways, I feel permanently homeless. In conversations with other first-generation "wanderers," I find this not uncommon. It seems to be less so for those who have children and grandchildren. For those who have stayed in one place.

My life experiences leave me deeply moved—awed even— by the diversity of the world and the beings that occupy it. I see clearly how we are all shaped by the ideas and ideals of language, culture, and relationships, by experiences and memories.

Even so, I often remind myself to be adaptable and open-minded.

IVY AND CARROTS

Once, after a long period of being apart, my father and I were spending some time together at my brother's cottage on Lake Erie. I had started my PhD program and was aware of how valuable my family history was. I had begun to record our conversations, wanting to preserve my father's and my own history. We were alone at these times. In the morning, after taking coffee, we would often walk the shore of lake as the sun was rising. He would wear his wooden shoes, clattering rhythmically on the road as we walked. Sometimes, we spoke; sometimes, we were silent and listened to the gulls and the rhythm of the waves. One morning, as we walked along the shore, my father suddenly fell silent for a long time.

Finally, he turned to me and asked, "Child, are you an ivy plant?"

I frowned, taken aback by the question. *What did he mean by that?*

Responding to my unspoken question, he continued, "Well, ivy plants are wanderers. They never stop. Go around one corner, and then another, and another."

Still frowning, I asked, "Dad, what should I be? What are you suggesting?"

"Could you ever consider being a carrot?" he quipped hopefully.

I looked at him in amazement and laughed. "Dad, the apple doesn't fall far from the tree. Look where you are!" After all, we were both a long way from Holland.

He was quiet for another moment and then pressed his point. "Ivy plants are travelers, they root in many places, their reach is wide, but their roots are shallow."

I took his veined hand in mine as we walked along in silence. I looked into his piercingly intelligent eyes and intuited what he might be thinking. He must have sensed what it was like to live my life of repeated relocation. He was a quiet man, brilliant, self-effacing, and endlessly curious. He had left much behind in Europe. As I look back from my own old age, I reflect that I may have unconsciously lived out some of his dreams as I traveled (often to military-governed countries, sometimes to countries at war) and explored the world. He had lived through two world wars; the stock market crash had taken him down, but he had rebuilt a family business. I thought of the things he might have done but couldn't as the eldest of thirteen and then the father of eight, his potential bandwidth bound to endless responsibility and urgency.

I was close to my dad. I saw him. I knew his gifted mind, moral depth, wisdom, and self-restraint. In my heart, I felt his loss and grief, his lost connections, the sacrifices he'd made. I knew the physical distance between us was painful for him. I, too, wished we lived closer.

On one of our last trips to the lake, he pulled out his beaten-up old wallet. A thin piece of parchment was folded inside. He opened it and put it on the table for me to read. It was Psalm 27. I knew it well and read it aloud with tears in my eyes. As we sat together, he looked at me and smiled. "You can have it when I am gone," he said, then carefully replaced it.

> The LORD is my light and my salvation; whom
> shall I fear? the LORD is the strength of my life;
> of whom shall I be afraid?

This verse stands out to me, even today as I think of his role in the war:

> Though a host should encamp against me, my
> heart shall not fear: though war should rise
> against me, in this will I be confident.

When I think of my dad and happiness, I think of Psalm 27. It was my father's ground. He was ever faithful to its words. When I think of Dad's *hedonic* happiness, I think of him eating dates, salted herring in onions, and "good potatoes." He was proud of his sons and the construction company they had created. He would spend entire days "at the shop," talking with the men, doing small chores, and feeding the dog. As he aged, he loved watching hockey and soccer on TV.

Above all, Dad loved to sleep in the sun. In his later years at Shalom, a home for seniors, he would lie down—on the grass, inside, wherever he could find a patch of sunlight. The staff was unsure as to what to do. In a family conference, they told my brother, "Mr. Demik sleeps on the floor!"

"In the sun?" Basil asked.

"Yes," they nodded.

"If that's okay, just let him be," Basil said. It was highly inappropriate, but so it was. People learned to walk around him as he rested with his bent arm as a pillow. While my mother had always been troubled by what neighbors might think, my father—to my mother's chagrin—cared little and had no interest or regard in social approval.

I never saw that piece of parchment again.

THE UNENDING ACHE OF HEIMSUCHUNG

Jenny Erpenbeck's 2008 novel, *Heimsuchung*, carries a title that resonates deeply with those of us who have left our homelands behind. *Heimsuchung* is a German word that translates to "home searching" and evokes a profound sadness, a longing for a place that can never be reclaimed. I call it the heart ache of a wanderer's life.

For me, heimsuchung is grief without closure, akin to mourning a child. It's difficult to explain to those who have never experienced it—a sense of falling out of time, of an interrupted bond that can never fully heal. For those who have experienced this displacement, the closure myth is just that—a myth.

I know I am not alone in this feeling of loss. Sometimes, when I am with friends from the Middle East, Central Soviet Asia, and the East, I look at the pictures on their walls. Their keepsakes, like mine, look like things from a museum—a collection of distant past artifacts disconnected from the present. This sense of displacement can be isolating and disorienting, a constant reminder of the life left behind.

Yet, there is also a strange beauty in heimsuchung, a bittersweet nostalgia for a time and place that exists only in memory. It's a reminder of the fragility of life, the impermanence of home, and the enduring power of connection to our roots.

THE PARADOX OF LONGING FOR
FREEDOM AND BELONGING

As a teenager, I was depressed. My mother and sister were both receiving electroshocks in the 1950s; my mother had cancer, and her colostomy and disfiguring rheumatoid arthritis left her in chronic pain, a permanent invalid. Survival was still a constant theme. Trying to make sense of my experiences, I turned to literature, among it, the existentialist writings of Camus, Kierkegaard, and Sartre, as well as survivors like Viktor Frankl.

During the tumultuous 1960s, I encountered Erich Fromm's intriguing idea that some of us may be content to escape the burden of responsibility that comes with freedom, that the structured life of authoritarian systems might be preferred to the chaos and uncertainty that comes with freedom of choice that returns with liberation.

As a family systems psychologist, this paradox resonates deeply with me. I've witnessed countless young people and families grapple with the desire for independence while simultaneously fearing the isolation and responsibility that comes with it. Some (and I was among them), like Pilgrim on his road to Beulah Land, get mired for a while in the sloughs of counter-dependence—fear of or refusal of help or intervention from parents and caretakers. Counter-dependence of "I don't need you; I'll do it alone" can leave kids prematurely independent, alone but unequipped for life's hard turning points. Interdependence, the rich fruit of the complex human journey, is not automatically found; it is a hard-earned journey cultivated by cooperation, effort, and sacrifice.

Freedom (the feeling of independence) grants us the opportunity to stand on our own two feet, to discover what we want and value, to shake off unwanted propping up and control of hierarchy, and to discard the constraints of shared obligations. Freedom as individualism can be a heady feeling of "it's all about me, about what I want and need, about doing it my way." It's heady, and it works for a while. While exhilarating, individualism is only a stop on the way, not meant to be a destination.

For a while, we prioritize autonomy and sacrifice community over self; we find ourselves less concerned with the well-being of others and less willing to extend a helping hand. In time, it no longer satisfies. Still enjoying the triumphs of freedom, we feel distressed, empty, and disconnected. A yearning for a sense of belonging to something larger than ourselves arises as the unfilled potential for interdependence, the hard-earned fruit of our interbeing, declares itself. We step up for the sacrifice, effort, and cultivation of interdependence, the balancing of our own needs with the needs of others. Freedom is now entangled with responsibility.

As a painter, when I mix blue and yellow to make a union in green, the two contributing colors are not deleted or erased; they have submitted to surrender, an amalgam, a sacrifice of self to create something new that combines both, into a "we." It may seem as if their presence is gone, but they are the constituents of green. They have been integrated but have not gone.

My brother John was two years older than I. As 8- and 10-year-olds, newly arrived in Canada, we were each other's sole playmates out in the "boondocks," miles from a small town called Schomberg. One day, we found a tree full of ripe cherries. John invited me to play a game.

"One for you, two for me. Two for you, three for me," he counted.

It took me a minute before I commented, "That's not fair. You're taking more!"

"Why are you doing that?" I asked.

My brother looked at me, his little sister, and said with a sly smile, "I can because I thought you wouldn't notice!"

He was joking and then quickly and warmly gave me my share. But it's more than a story!

In clinical practice, such stories illustrate predation and perpetration of the quality of meeting our individual needs at someone else's expense.

While my brother was teasing and being playful, we all have experience with individuals who claim more assets or contribute less time and effort than others. Some, like young children, do not experience a sense of responsibility or obligation to reciprocate. When such behavior is called out, it generates a response not of guilt or shame but elicits anger, a conviction of having been unfairly victimized by the person who calls it out. This feeling of being entitled to gain more and contribute less is often called narcissism. It's customary in young children.

If our development stops in the stage of self-absorption or individualism, we risk isolation, find ourselves in shallow relationships, cut off from the deep bonds of connection that give our lives meaning and purpose. As we mature, we realize that compromise and cooperation, the glue that holds communities together, are often messy and imperfect.

Tolerance for complexity, of "both/and" rather than only "either/or," is a hallmark of maturity. It requires understanding and acceptance of giving and taking, receiving and extending. We live in an interconnected tapestry, the warp and weft of moral fibers that weave us together as both individuals and members of the collective.

RECLAIMING THE ROOTS OF BELONGING

I'm retired now, but when I think back on my days in clinical practice, I remember those moments when I'd "feel people" upon first meeting them, an inadvertent intuitive sense. My first session with Kyle was like that. He "felt" flat but boastful—full of himself, yet hollow. While I often felt immediate warmth with folks, with Kyle, I felt myself pulling back, matching and mirroring his distancing.

He introduced himself: name, age, address, the name of his university, and—quickly added—the name of his fraternity. It was like an ad for a "frat." A young man, his heart buried under layers of status signals, ambitions, and the "right" attire, pressured by fraternity expectations, insecure, distant. The first few sessions, he didn't feel real. I sensed a screaming need for external validation; he seemed to measure his worth by accolades, material success, by inspiring envy in his mates.

To my surprise, on the third session, he shifted and pivoted. With vulnerable candor, he opened the session by telling me, "I know I'm a prick! The truth is, I feel like shit about myself. I cover it up, but I think I'm a fraud. The truth is, I don't fit in. I don't feel like I belong anywhere."

His transparency stunned me for a moment. I made eye contact, smiled, nodded. "How about we start there today?" I asked. He nodded yes, and we started our work.

I soon grew to like Kyle, deeply motivated to help him figure it out. I was moved by his willingness to be unguarded, to let me in. I felt his resolve to be real, to uncover what he was really experiencing. We could meet each other there and do meaningful work.

A breakthrough came one day when our conversation sparked Kyle's childhood memory of building sandcastles on the beach with his father—a moment when his often-impatient father was tender and playful. The memory was bittersweet, tinged with his father's frequent emotional absence, but it also evoked a sense of joy and uncomplicated love.

"He saw me, he was so there with me," Kyle said, tears welling in his eyes as he recounted the moment of sweet connection. "It was worth a year of my life," he said, stumbling on the words as he wept. "It was a moment he approved. He loved my castle and added a new wing on the castle with me. He said I could be a great builder, an architect."

I saw that it had been a rare moment of validation. My eyes filled with tears as I thought of how much the young boy had needed his dad and of how infrequent those important encounters had been.

The work deepened after that day. As trust increased, he was more willing to risk, to be vulnerable, to talk not only of his vainglorious accomplishments but of his fears, his shame, his doubt about his own worthiness. The vacuous fragility I had sensed initially was being replaced by something grounded. I felt his growing confidence in who he was, and the increase in healthy self-approval. In time, he dropped some of the masks he had used as shields. As he dared to be authentic, he saw how common and human his fears were. As he peeled back the veils of shame and fear, he was able to share his frequent "self-loathing." His braggadocious armor fell away as he no longer felt he needed it.

Kyle joined a men's therapy group. He started to date a woman he was attracted to, not because she was "hot eye candy" or something he could brag about. As he became more vulnerable and authentic, his ego needs changed. More comfortable with himself, he released the empty self-promotion that had never served him. He became more real, open, able to be honest, someone others sought out for friendship.

Much of my work as a clinician has been "deep work." Instead of dealing with and finding ways to cope with short-term crises or short-term interventions, the conversations have often been about life's foundational questions: existential concerns, broad philosophical questions related to the meaning and purpose of life, the human condition, isolation, responsibility, the burden of freedom of choice, existential anxiety, meaninglessness, and death. Many of my clients had suffered deep wounds and injuries that evoke these kinds of feelings and concerns.

So, how *does* the heart find happiness? How can we find and walk the road of authenticity, interconnection, and belonging?

FREEDOM, FEAR, AND THE PRICE OF TRUTH

To express oneself authentically often means stepping out of line, ruffling feathers, and challenging the prevailing winds of popular opinion. It means risking disapproval, ostracism, and even the loss of status and favor. It means inviting accusations of rudeness or aggression. Saying "no" can be resistance to what seems wrong or immoral.

Boundaries are limits that arise from conviction. To speak or not to speak, even to have an opinion or to care enough to speak, arises from tension, a tension of choice that mirrors the broader struggle between freedom and fear, between the desire for authenticity and the comfort of conformity, the desire to belong and the risk of expulsion.

They say the Dutch are blunt. As someone with a healthy dose of Dutch heritage coursing through my veins, I feel this cultural quirk whenever my "Dutch bluntness" collides with the "Minnesota nice" of my adopted home. The difference isn't always harmonious. However uncomfortable, I prefer "plain truth." For me, placating expressions quickly land as subtle evasion, leaving me unsure of where someone stands.

Call it a character flaw, but I'd rather risk the sting of crude honesty than the allure of conflict avoidance. As they say, freedom isn't free, and the price of speaking one's mind— of daring to declare the emperor's nakedness, daring to set limits—can be steep indeed. We need limits and boundaries to regulate emotions, and preserve balance. Without limits, personal preferences and control can infringe and do harm to others.

I was alone in the hospital healing from a fall when Trump was reelected. My sister Nelly (who lives in Michigan) and I had shared news stories for months. We were both remembering, reminding each other of what we had witnessed: Hitler's steps to power in the 1930s. Eighty years later, it felt like bookends folding together—in one lifetime.

Around that time, I braced when a friend chirped brightly, "Oh, I just go with the flow. Everyone is different. I accept where people are."

Her words stopped me as if I had been hit. I felt immediate anger. I intuited that she prided herself in being "easygoing" and that for her, "going along" was virtue signaling that served the casual purpose of a bromide, that it was meant to placate.

Her self-described easygoing way troubled me. Conditioned by the harsh realities of my childhood, what she said sounded pseudo-innocent. I reacted internally. *You seem happy to be free of judgment. You live in a world of privilege, but what if you were not so fortunate? What if you saw someone being abused? What if you were being abused? Would you then so cheerfully go with the flow?*

I did not speak these words. I intuited that I had encountered a misunderstanding about "going with the flow." The acceptance it seemed to point to is not about blindly acquiescing to everything that comes our way or becoming a neutral bystander for whatever someone wants to do or feel. It goes deeper. Acceptance is about recognizing what is without judgment, but that doesn't mean we don't resist anything or that we condone everything.

I learned early that there are roads love won't take. There are times when going with the flow is collusion and collaboration, consent—a way of avoiding responsibility. Sometimes, the path requires us to stand up and say "no."

Going with the flow means more than one thing; it can mean moving toward what is wholesome, life-affirming, and *away* from what causes harm. It's like a river navigating obstacles, finding its way to the sea.

My childhood experiences have sharpened my awareness of suffering and injustice. It's a sometimes troublesome gift of awareness that comes with anger and frustration; it evokes a responsibility to speak out when you see harm being done. Sometimes too bluntly to do good.

I've learned that direct or blunt, spontaneous responses are not always the most skillful. It works in Holland, in groups where confrontation is part of the norm, but in other cultures, people may be deeply wounded and react defensively to any perceived criticism. Seeing oneself as a victim of an attack does nothing to promote deeper awareness.

At some point in life, we all face this divide—the delicate balance between expressing our truths and respecting the sensitivities of others. The willingness to risk speaking up for what is right is a powerful force for good in the world. We can seek to find a way to balance our inner compass's voice with the needs of others. Practice and compassion make this possible.

THE APPEAL AND PERIL OF POSITIVITY

Most of us would prefer to be positive, to give supportive help and feedback. A positive attitude is often rightfully lauded for fostering openness, flexibility, and an optimistic outlook. However, there exists a darker side to this virtuous trait. Positivism can be an "easy out," a tool for willful ignorance, a means to turn a blind eye to wrongdoing in the pursuit of comfort and conflict avoidance. When positivism takes the form of people-pleasing as a means to ensure being liked or to belong, it can sanctify injustice, unfairness, and harmful behaviors.

When morality is sacrificed on the altar of rewards—gaining the benefits of being considered loyal, upbeat, pleasant, and compliant—we are on a slippery slope of collaborating with harm. Such choices were frequently made in my childhood, as many capitulated to the Nazi occupation and withdrew, allowing abuse and harm to go unchecked. A lack of accountability breeds a silent acceptance of wrong. It's akin to the emperor's new clothes, where everyone refuses to acknowledge the obvious truth.

There are always those who dare to dissent, see through the facade, and speak up against injustice. These outliers often stand alone, embodying moral resistance. They may face rejection and ridicule, but their unwavering commitment to truth is crucial for social progress.

THE DANGERS OF TOXIC POSITIVITY

In the real world, negative emotions like sadness, anger, and fear cannot simply be reframed away. They demand acknowledgment and processing. Telling someone to "just think positive" invalidates their feelings and can lead to isolation and a lack of support. Positivity is found in dysfunctional families when parents want to play "let's pretend." Pretending that abuse isn't happening to "keep the peace." Yet it's a false peace that can be toxic.

As a family therapist, I often met clients who came from families where negativity was not permitted. More than once, I met with someone who declared that they had never seen the expression of anger between parents! Needless to say, these individuals had anger issues, sometimes unable to be aware of the emotion of anger even when the body was expressing it in physical symptoms.

I think of Nancy, a middle-aged woman with an unwavering belief in the power of positivity. She prided herself on reframing every negative experience into a positive one, a kind of Pollyanna thinking, avoiding conflict at all costs. While her intentions were good, her refusal to acknowledge negativity became a form of self-deception.

Nancy's positivity, upon closer examination, masked a fear of tension and a deep-seated need for approval. It was a learned coping mechanism, a way to bypass the discomfort of confrontation.

"My father thought it would reflect on him, so we always had to spin things positively," Nancy told me. It took much support, encouragement, time, and work before she believed it was okay to allow those feelings to surface, before she was able to share her sadness, pain, grief, and other human emotions that had been disapproved of and forbidden.

The belief that everything can be framed positively is unrealistic and sets the stage for disappointment. Life is a tapestry of both positive and negative experiences. Challenging and painful events, while unpleasant, often provide valuable opportunities for growth and self-discovery.

Refusing to acknowledge problems doesn't make them disappear. It can exacerbate them. Ignoring issues can be a reckless evasion of responsibility, a lack of moral courage, or a resort to mere cowardice.

BALANCING POSITIVITY AND REALISM

A healthy approach to life involves acknowledging and processing negative emotions while maintaining a hopeful outlook. It's about finding a balance between positivity and realism.

Toxic positivity, emphasis on one pole with disregard for the other, can be a ready form of denial. A similar, related option arises in the form of spiritual bypassing, or the use of spiritual practices to avoid dealing with difficult emotions or situations. Both constitute a refusal to engage with the complexities of life, a way to shield oneself from discomfort. Toxic positivity and spiritual bypassing can readily arise in individuals called "snowflakes" today, referring to those who have been shielded from many life hardships and are easily overwhelmed by even minor inconveniences when they manifest.

There is a time and place for everything, including willful ignorance. However, looking away is not neutral and has consequences in times of crisis and injustice. To those who only want to know the positive, a reminder to consider the fates of those facing oppression and hardship, like the people of Ukraine or Gaza, may be well advised.

Pollyanna thinking, toxic positivity, and spiritual bypassing can convince their believers that the evil they experience is temporary and passing. People with these mindsets choose to be unaware of unpleasant things that are real. But that choice is fundamentally one-sided, and a means of avoiding the reality that not everyone is concerned about the welfare of others.

Unrealistic optimism (like willful ignorance) chooses not to see based on its own requirements for sustaining its lighthearted life view. It chooses to see evil as smoke that simply disappears, choosing not to imagine what it's like to be hungry, unhoused, a child sex toy, or a child soldier. It refuses to expand enough to hold, integrate, and transcend the light and the dark. Optimism has its place; there are times when looking through its lens allows us the lift we need to get through hard times.

Evil and good both start as small seeds with phenomenal potential. Both are contagious, and like an infection, can spread like wildfire when left unchecked. Likewise, hatred and gossip have inklike power. All it takes is one drop to change what it falls on.

I watch TV with a new friend. There is a clip of a documentary and a photo of Dachau. She looks away and explains she is too fragile; it is just too difficult for her to know these things. I see something else. I see unwillingness to feel the pain others bear, unwillingness to be tainted by the reality of life she doesn't want to know or experience—a reality others live in and suffer daily from.

I feel my contempt, disdain, and hate. I know I am triggered. I want to get away from her ignorance and the dangerous limitations that she appears to defend without shame. I am aware of my reaction.

I try to find my compassion, to find the antidote to what I am feeling. I'm sure she could, on the spot, give me a little sermon on how what I am feeling is destructive. I could give myself the same sermon.

Under it all: my own pain.

She has an innocent view that I and those like me have lost and never had time to acquire.

As a young child, I wanted to believe in the power of good. I wanted to believe that life was fair. When I looked at the world I lived in, I saw no evidence of it. While my family survived, I saw others who did not. While my father was not tortured, I knew those who were. Cruelty and evil are not just ideas. They are as real as a tree or a door. I witnessed them. Many who had believed in good at the start of the war still did at the end of the war, but they also believed in the reality of evil.

Evil had lived next-door in the neighborhood, clubbing to death the man in front of our house, the men shot in the village, the men who were taken away. Some of us would not—not ever for fun—shoot a rabbit or a squirrel. Others in the village shot people, hunted people, like the British hunt fox. For sport. They met innocent eyes with a bullet or a club.

The heart can be a dangerous thing. It is not true that people always get what they deserve. Bad things happen to good people, as Rabbi Kushner notes. And it is not true that we can always change our fates with our attitude. But it is true that even in the worst of times when we have no control over our fates, we still have control over how we manage it. As Viktor Frankl wrote in *Man's Search for Meaning*, we can choose how we respond or resist, even in the worst circumstances.

Today in our privileged world, there are many who have not directly experienced that evil walks in the world right next to the good, silently threading its carpet like a spider's web—often seen only when it's too late.

> There is no need to fear evil. There is every need
> to understand what it does, how it operates in the
> world, what it draws upon to sustain itself. We must
> not shrink from the knowledge of the evilness of evil.
>
> *Howard Thurman*

Heart Questions

1. What kind of happiness do you tend to seek? How do you balance a need for hedonic and eudaimonic happiness?

2. Think about your "roots of belonging." If you've been a carrot, how might it feel to be an ivy? Where might you go? How might it feel to have deep, long-standing roots if you're ivy?

3. What is your experience of a need for belonging or desires for happiness or positivity? Has either affected your capacity to discern between good and evil?

Chapter 10

Choosing Self-Worth and Authenticity

Our deepest calling is to grow into our own
authentic self-hood, whether or not it conforms
to some image of who we ought to be. As
we do so, we will not only find the joy that
every human being seeks—we will also find
our path of authentic service in the world.

Parker J. Palmer

———

HOW WE PERCEIVE ourselves (our sense of self-image) profoundly impacts our hearts, actions, and how we present
ourselves to the world. A recent conversation with a dear
friend, who gently pointed out my tendency to name-drop,
prompted a deep introspection into my own sense of self,
class, and place in the hierarchy of how our culture per-
ceives the world.

Reflecting on my friend's observation led me to revisit
old memories, tracing the roots of my self-image back to
my childhood. In Canada in the 1950s, the mandatory education ended at age 16. The youngest of my brothers (Pete
and John) had to leave school at that young age to help support our family. For my elder brother, Basil, and my sisters
(Betsy, Nelly, Audrey, and Etha), educational opportunities
had been cut short—and closed—by the war. My brothers
followed in my father's footsteps, working in construction.

As a teen, I was blond-haired, blue-eyed, five-foot-five (a little bigger than the desirable five-foot-two, per the then-popular Bing Crosby song), and I had only one skirt. I remember wishing I could have clothes like other girls were wearing. To my surprise, two years after we moved to Hamilton (the city), my brother Pete surprised me by purchasing another skirt so I could take turns.

It was the way life was. I never felt victimized or short-changed. Survival, being able to fit in at school and make it, was its own reward. On a community level, I affiliated only with other Dutch immigrants in the same survival ballpark.

A pivotal moment occurred when Basil was laid off. This ending marked a new beginning, as my father and brothers joined forces to start their own construction company, Demik Construction. (My family, following in the footsteps of other immigrants, had changed their name from de Mik to Demik. First names were also changed to English equivalents. I remember the first day of grade 5—once again in a new school—the teacher read off our names. When she read mine, Leentje—Leni is a diminutive of Leentje, like Tom and Thomas or Mike and Michael—I stood up and said, "That's not my name; my name is Elaine." That evening, I announced my new name to my family. No one objected, and it was legally changed to Elaine when I became a Canadian citizen. Years later, at the time of my divorce, I changed my last name from my husband's back to my father's and reclaimed my original name, Leni. I preferred Leni de Mik.)

I vividly recall the evenings when my younger brother, brimming with excitement, would share the company's latest project offers. "We are building a gas station for Esso," he'd exclaim. "We are the only company working for Esso in our city!" These conversations, filled with astonishment and well-deserved pride, resonated deeply with me. I was so proud of them! They were achieving some status in the community, and status counted!

I shared his elation, recognizing his underlying message: "Can you believe it? Me, an uneducated immigrant kid, entrusted with something so far beyond my expectations!" I witnessed firsthand the transformation of self-image, from humble beginnings to newfound confidence and accomplishment.

I recall another time in the 1960s, when, coming from my background and culture, I tried to adapt and fit in with the cultured intelligentsia of Munich. I watched myself faking it, trying to appear authentic as if I were an actress in a movie scene. I knew I could quickly get busted as an imposter. During that time, I often spent Sunday afternoons in a chalet in the Alps with a family of one of the directors at Krupp, a large German industrial company. The son of that family, whom I'll call Peter, was a physicist and a colleague of my then-husband at the Max Planck Institute and would invite us to his parents' chalet for weekends.

It was an unknown elegance for me. I was totally out of my league. One room in the chalet was dedicated to listening to music. Peter would ask me what piece I would like to hear. That was bad enough, although I could always come up with something from Beethoven, Mahler, or Tchaikovsky. But I would silently shake in my shoes when he followed with a question about which director I would like to hear. I had no idea. I knew nothing about music, but I could approximate how I felt I *should be* if I possessed that culture.

It's a great relief to no longer suffer from that need to "play act," but rather to feel natural and authentic, unashamed now that I don't know something when I don't.

Fast forward to that recent conversation with my friend: as I stood in my yard with my neighbor, excitedly sharing about a new project, I noticed myself highlighting the prestigious details, the status, and the wealth of my collaborator. It struck me then: Am I bragging? Even though I'd like to believe I'm above such "juvenile" behavior, it's a humble realization. Something in me needs to let people know that I am someone. Being associated with "people of status" lets people know that I count; I matter. Perhaps it was a piece of psychological shrapnel from being chronically outranked by siblings who "knew more" and had more experience and power than I had as the youngest.

This experience highlighted the enduring presence of my early self-image, the Cinderella within. Despite the new image I've constructed through life experiences, that younger sense of self, the contrast between who I was and who I am now, remains alive and entangled with my present life. It still holds the power to move me.

While I may have evolved and transcended that earlier self-image, my friend's observation revealed how it still shapes my interactions and reactions. It's a reminder that our past experiences, particularly those that shape our self-perception, leave lasting imprints on our hearts and minds.

We are social beings with a deeply ingrained need to belong and be accepted by others. To belong is to feel seen, heard, and valued. To belong is to think more clearly, walk taller, and speak with a sense of authority. Hopefully, it is a stance that does not claim the kind of authority that rules over others but the kind that comes directly from the heart.

But here's the catch: Belonging is not only about fitting in; it's about showing up. It's what one of my teachers calls walking as well as talking the game, hopefully with a clear understanding of who you are and a sincere resolve to meet the moment. Showing up this way is not simple; it requires an alchemical fusion of purpose, self-acceptance, and deep connections.

> The worst loneliness is to not be
> comfortable with yourself.
>
> *Mark Twain*

AWARENESS IS AN INNER PATH OF SELF-DISCOVERY

Cultivating a self-aware heart is a lifelong practice we must return to again and again. Self-awareness is a process that asks things of us and requires us to make conscious choices. It calls us to lay down our defenses and look at ourselves as we are, through transparent windows, to re-examine the stories we tell ourselves and the narratives we live by.

Self-awareness allows us to understand our character, motivations, feelings, strengths, and weaknesses. It involves seeing ourselves objectively, to be aware of how our actions impact others. It includes understanding our inner values, thoughts, emotions, and insights into how others perceive us. While self-awareness seems like a no-brainer, it is uncommon and elusive. For many, it is barely present, undeveloped, or truncated. When cultivated and consciously practiced, self-awareness provides us with "in sight," an inspiration to open our lives to new pathways, to choose something different, and to create new narratives.

Now, step by step, possibilities rise up to greet us. Armed with courage and self-esteem, we accept accountability and the ability to face our vulnerabilities without shame. We begin to deconstruct the old restricting dualities of identity: good or bad, successful or failure, adequate or inadequate, loving or mean, kind or unkind. A new capacity to hold the tension of opposites opens us to unconditional acceptance, enabling us to accept ourselves as all that we are.

This fundamental core of acceptance becomes the new ground. We grow in our willingness and ability to accept responsibility and accountability. As the heart opens to our vulnerabilities and limitations, we can extend the same to others.

We recognize that, like all things, we are beings shaped in an ongoing process of formation and transformation, ever evolving and changing. Ever accountable for our choices.

IS SELF-AWARENESS COMMONPLACE?

We assume self-awareness is commonplace, but studies have found it is surprisingly rare. Although self-awareness is linked to numerous benefits, such as decision-making, relationship strength, confidence, and leadership success, studies suggest that it's rarer than we'd like to believe. Organizational psychologist Tasha Eurich found in her research that 95% of people believe they are self-aware, but only 10–15% fit the criteria— because there is a difference between internal and external self-awareness. We might be aware of our values, aspirations, and personality strengths and weaknesses, but oblivious to how others see us on the same attributes (or vice versa).[23]

Why might this be? There may be many reasons to explain why we may choose not to know ourselves deeply (we'll consider willful ignorance next). While self-awareness is an

---

23 Tasha Eurich, "What Self-Awareness Really Is (and How to Cultivate It)," *Harvard Business Review*, January 4, 2018, https://hbr. org/2018/01/what-self-awareness-really-is-and-how-to-cultivate-it,

objective appraisal devoid of self-criticism and judgment, it can conflict with our ideal self-image, making us uncomfortable and vulnerable. Rather than choosing to expose the chinks in the armor of our idealized self, we may select to hide and soften the unacceptable features, denying the parts we don't want to own, in the comfort of not knowing.

In my clinical and personal experience, I see a strong link between self-awareness and comfort with vulnerability, as mentioned earlier. We humans have a way of creating walls around "flaws" to protect our ego from negative feedback that leaves us feeling exposed and vulnerable. We create walls and close doors, building elaborate defenses like denial, minimization, and rationalization, to protect against uncomfortable exposure. Often, we project them onto others as a way of seeing those defenses, but not in ourselves. Our unwillingness can, in time, lead us to overestimate our abilities. It may leave us quick to react defensively, have difficulty hearing and accepting constructive criticism, and blind us to our actions and their impact and consequences on others.

Self-awareness grows as we gain courage and become more comfortable with vulnerability. As we grow in our encounters with our "disowned" and "not nice" parts, we can begin to integrate them. Practice makes possible, and as our sense of who we are becomes more authentic, a more transparent view of ourselves arises. That upgrade in self-awareness becomes a strength, allowing us to make choices more in alignment with who we are, with what matters to us.

THE THREE MONKEYS OF WILLFUL IGNORANCE

Willful ignorance is akin to a lack of self-awareness—how often are we aware of what we're (subconsciously or consciously) choosing to ignore? Linh Vu and Margarita Leib, two behavioral scientists in the Netherlands, studied ethical decision-making. They examined why some people decide "not to know" and how "not knowing or willful ignorance" can free people to act selfishly. It reminds me of the three monkeys who see no evil, hear no evil, and speak no evil—the epitome of willful ignorance. Vu and Leib's research suggests that people, at least in part, may choose ignorance to shield themselves from their own self-judgment. They opine that claims of ignorance may protect us from knowing how our actions harm others and prevent us from feeling value discordance. Such behavior is seen, for example, in people unwilling to understand the impact of climate change. As one of my friends sheepishly admitted, "I love my long showers, I love a good steak, I don't want to think about chickens in cages all of their lives. I don't want to feel guilty, change my lifestyle." Many of us avoid looking too intently at the production process behind the convenience products we purchase daily. Willful ignorance is not innocence. It enables corruption in industries, politics, and business.

"If we can avoid putting a strong moral emphasis on decisions, it may make people feel less threatened and, as a result, be less willfully ignorant," wrote the researchers in an article for *Scientific American*. Inspiring rather than guilting people into more ethical or altruistic choices is more likely to succeed. "In short, we can encourage one another and ourselves toward more selfless and generous actions."[24]

We all have the power to create and live an authentic life, a power that comes from our choices and capacity for self-awareness. When we own our unique qualities, quirks, and

---

24 Linh Vu and Margarita Leib, "Why Some People Choose Not to Know," *Scientific American* 330, no. 4 (April 2024): 76, http://doi.org/10.1038/scientificamerican0424-76.

values, and their reflection in our actions, speech, and decisions, we experience the fullness of an authentic life. Rather than willfully hiding behind the opinions and judgments of others or self-shaming, we can show up as our own unique selves and live the life we are called to live.

> Your level of belonging, in fact, can never be greater than your level of self-acceptance, because believing that you're enough is what gives you the courage to be authentic, vulnerable and imperfect.
>
> *Brené Brown*

FROM SAFE SPACE TO HEART SPACE

We all need to belong and feel accepted by our "tribe." To leave and self-exile, or to be exiled and cast out from our foundational social groups, threatens our sense of being safe in knowing that we are not alone and that others have our back. But not all can remain in the groups they are born into. For various reasons, continued connection can be or seems impossible. How do we respond when our deeply ingrained need to belong and be accepted by others threatens our safety or the safety of our family?

During the COVID pandemic, obeying rules designed to contain the virus spread took the forefront of attention and became a virtue for many. Families sheltered in place with each other. However, as many as one out of four Americans had no family connection to shelter with. The fact that "shelter in place" left these individuals isolated gained little attention. While the surgeon general Vivek Murthy clarified that loneliness and isolation are significant physical and mental health risks, the order to contain the viral spread by staying at home appeared to override the concern for those with no family support. Fear of death by exposure took the forefront and overshadowed the risk of demise by isolation.

It troubled me and brought back memories of war—of those who had been isolated and hunted. I remembered those who had not looked away, who had noticed, risking their lives to save others. I remembered the days of accounting after the war, when choices had been questioned.

I remembered other times—the 1960s and '70s—when rules had been broken: The civil rights marches, farm worker strikes, the women's movement, and the Vietnam War resisters who went to prison rather than serve in what they felt was an unjust war. I thought of ideals about sacrifice, compassion, and the common good. During the pandemic, they seemed no longer well-defined. For some, meeting the moment meant strictly abiding by regulated mandates; for others, it was less clear. As in the war, some broke the rules for a higher good.

During the shelter-in-place mandate, I received a call from my friend Katherine, who still goes daily to a shelter where I also frequently volunteer. She told me about a guest at the shelter who was in deep despair. This guest, whom I will call Gail, was suicidal. Katherine wondered if I'd be willing to meet with her.

Katherine and I went together to see Gail. After an introduction, Katherine stepped away to give us some privacy. I learned that Gail had recently moved to Minneapolis. She had lost both parents in the last three years. Her sister had died unexpectedly six months ago and her best friend three months ago. Three weeks earlier, her only child had died by suicide.

Gail lived alone in a building where everyone walked through the hallways masked and distancing. I promised to use my influence to set up some support for her. She was grateful. So was I.

As our conversation ended, Katherine returned. We said our goodbyes and I started off. When Katherine didn't follow, I turned back and saw Katherine, masked, put her arms around Gail and hold her. I saw Gail's body soften as she leaned into the embrace. Tears flowed down her cheek.

"I will quarantine," Katherine said, as she joined me.

The following day, I checked in with Gail on the phone. She told me she had slept for the first time in many days. She paused, and then added, "I know I should not have hugged Katherine. But it helped so much. It was the first time I was touched since my son died."

Authentic connection made a difference.

CONFRONTING COMPLEXITY WITH COURAGE

What too often gets in the way of authentic connection is our relationship to differences. Differences become points of division.

It's a paradox. Differences—the spectrum of threads that create the many patterns in the rich tapestry of humanity—are often twisted, reactively, into wedges of separation. It leaves us clinging to tribal lines in the sand, endless arguments over beliefs and perceptions of what is right and what is wrong.

In his poem "Song of Myself," Walt Whitman reminds us, "I am large, I contain multitudes." Humanity is like that: it offers a mosaic of experiences, perspectives, and identities. Denying differences is to deny the fullness of our shared humanity. Authentic unity consists not of homogeneity but of embracing the fullness of that spectrum.

Wisdom, self-awareness, and acceptance are the properties that allow us to bridge the divides, to sweep away the boundaries we create that then needlessly divide and separate us. And that takes courage.

Courage is not the absence of fear but the audacity to confront it. Courage is a choice: Courage tells us not to follow the script of evolution, not to flee what scares us, but to pivot and walk into the unknown. Courage is the willingness to face the unknown, to confront the shadows lurking in our mind's dark corners. Courage reveals that healing a broken, traumatized heart is not finding a way to eradicate scars but a way to transform wounds into sources of strength and wisdom. Courage finds a way to claim what was lost, to release constraints that bind us and keep us from igniting our innate potential. Courage allows us to rekindle, renew, and cultivate our connection with the person we can be.

Courage gained from the fertile soil of love empowers us to speak truth to power, challenge injustice, and strive for a better world. The quiet whispers of a courageous heart remind us that we are enough and already have what it takes to navigate the complexities of life.

Nature, art, and meaningful work all offer paths to a courageous heart. With its enduring cycles, the natural world can remind us of the resilience of all life, even when our heart throbs with the raw pain of existence. Art can speak what cannot be articulated in words. Since early childhood, painting has allowed me to express the unspeakable. The peace I knew must exist despite the existential trauma of my childhood would show up on the canvas where river and land flowed, where the storms in my mind loomed darkly over sunlit valleys. In painting, I found my voice, my creative courage. My emotions found expression as canvas met my brush, hard, thrusting, in the untamed display of turbulent color that tore through the quiet of the canvas.

These untamed childhood experiences gave me a glimpse of what I learned later; that meaningful work can express and renew our sense of purpose, infuse us with inspiration, and allow us to contribute to something larger than ourselves.

It's not a straightforward journey, and setbacks are part of the process. Like the breath, waves rise and recede. As we lose and then rediscover our courageous hearts, our connection with ourselves, others, and the world is restored. Between all the hurdles, obstacles, and setbacks, we evolve and bloom like dandelions breaking through concrete.

BETWEEN RIVER AND LAND

When I was growing up, there were sometimes heated, controversial conversations between my older siblings. These conversations tended to be tension points, with one sibling choosing one point of view while the other took the opposing view. My father would grow impatient and say, "*Tussen rivier en landt*," which translates to "between river and land."

It was perplexing. It meant something to him but I didn't get it.

A small stream from the larger river flowed at the edge of our land 30 yards from our house, and I would try to imagine such a place. Years later, I finally asked him what it meant.

"It isn't a real place. It's an imaginary position, a vantage point, from which you can see both sides—and then decide what matters," Dad paused for a moment before continuing, "If you only know the river, how can you help folks who live on the land? If you only know land, how can you find a solution that works for everyone?" Dad even reminded me how my uncle Bas discovered that for him, living on "the Ark" (his river boat) best fit his needs.

I now know Dad was pointing out that the answers to life's complicated, hard questions are often not found in polarities or opposites. The best direction is often found neither on land nor river. Creative solutions, unexpected openings, often arise when land and river are held together in the tension of both/and. We must transcend the simple truths of childhood to embrace greater complexity. Just as we have come to understand that technologies like microscopes, telescopes, and MRIs allow us views deeper and more complex than the human eye can provide, we come to understand that increased mental capacity for complexity can give us different views of the world, of existence, of life itself.

My mind frequently turns back to that conversation with my dad when I think about how we all contribute to and are influenced by our culture, and how our culture, in turn, influences our beliefs about what is and isn't acceptable—about right and wrong, about who's right and who's wrong.

A TIME FOR COMPASSION

The war ended after five years of terror, starvation, and unimaginable cruelty and an estimated 50 million civilian and 25 million military deaths. For days, the men in the defeated German army moved slowly out of our village alongside their battered tanks. They walked along the street, which in the Netherlands was also the top the *dijk*. One afternoon, I climbed up the steep hill to watch their retreat. When I reached the top, the river of men had stopped to rest. One of them saw me and asked me for water.

I ran down the hill and filled the special red bucket the milkman had once used to deliver milk. I filled it as full as possible, then headed back up the steep hill. My mother ran from our home, yelling for me to stop. She caught up to me, grabbed my arm, and squeezed until I dropped the bucket. "We don't give water to the enemy," she said in a cold, stern voice.

Then she turned toward the river of soldiers. She watched for a long time, then took the bucket from my hand and offered the pail to the waiting soldier I was meeting. He drank, passed the bucket to another, then another. When it was empty, the soldiers quietly said, "*Dank u well*" in Dutch and handed the bucket back.

Mother locked eyes with each man, nodded, and turned away, then took my hand gently. Together, we walked down the hill.

"Jan," she said quietly to my father, who had been watching from below, "most of them look like children."

There were indeed children among those retreating troops. Boys as young as 12 had been drafted into the war at its end in 1945. In subsequent days as Nazi evacuation continued, Mother sometimes suggested that I walk up the hill to offer the soldiers water. That moment on the slope had changed her. Like the young soldier who'd spared the lives of a starving family, her heart opened—and five years of mind-numbing fear dissolved into compassion.

Later, I understood even more deeply what my father had been trying to teach me. While it seems paradoxical, there is a way to realize that the river and the land represent choices. That we are essentially neither good nor evil. We have the capacity for both: for good *and* evil, for kindness *and* cruelty, for greed *and* generosity. In my spiritual quest, I understand that when we learn to look inside without judgment, we discover this potential for choice that lives inside all of us and that comes to define us. We can choose good when we recognize and manage this duality with awareness and intention.

I keep thinking of David Bohm's ideas of folding and unfolding, constructing and deconstructing what we consider reality. We are—each and all of us—a river flowing, constantly folding and unfolding, manifesting as form, as land and substance, and dissolving, returning to the river, the flow, the yin and yang dance of form and formlessness.

> Even a wounded world is feeding us. Even a wounded world holds us, giving us moments of wonder and joy. I choose joy over despair. Not because I have my head in the sand, but because joy is what the earth gives me daily and I must return the gift.
>
> *Robin Wall Kimmerer*

Heart Questions

1. What comes to mind about your own struggle to bridge the gap between what you aspire to be and who you truly are?

2. In what areas of your life might you be consciously or subconsciously choosing "not to know," and how might confronting this willful ignorance foster greater self-worth and a more authentic expression of yourself?

3. Find somewhere to experience standing "between river and land" in person—ideally more than once, over the seasons. What do you notice in the embodied metaphor?

PART III

Alchemy of an Undivided Heart

The river needs to take the risk
of entering the ocean
because only then will fear disappear,
because that's where the river will know
it's not about disappearing into the ocean,
but of becoming the ocean.

Kahlil Gibran, from "Fear"

Chapter 11

Connecting Through Non-Dual Compassion

In nature nothing is at a standstill, everything
pulsates, appears and disappears. Heart,
breath, digestion, sleep and waking—birth
and death—everything comes and goes
in waves. Rhythm, periodicity, harmonious
alternation of extremes is the rule. No use
rebelling against the very pattern of life.

Nisargadatta Maharaj

———

IN THE AFTERMATH of war, amidst the rubble and the echoes of trauma, my father fashioned a teeter-totter from a simple plank and a fulcrum. This makeshift contraption, a child's plaything born of scarcity, became my first classroom of life's most profound lessons.

On that seesaw, I learned about duality—the interplay of up and down, the constant negotiation of balance. I felt the thrill of power as I held my playmate suspended in mid-air and the vulnerability of being held aloft, feet dangling, unmoored. The teeter-totter taught me about tension, about choice, about the extremes of control and surrender.

In the liminal space between earth and sky, I glimpsed the paradoxical nature of existence—the ambiguity, the contra-dictions. Everything I later learned about non-duality, about the interconnectedness of seemingly disparate forces, found its roots in those childhood moments on the teeter-totter. Of course I could not have named these themes back then. The lessons of the teeter-totter were primitive, arising from a child's mind with its simple opposites of up and down, with little nuance or complexity.

The teeter-totter, with its rhythmic ups and downs, mirrors the heart's delicate balance of giving and receiving love. Just as the teeter-totter needs participants on both sides for it to work, a healthy heart requires both the ability to give love generously and to receive it openly.

The upward swing is the heart's ability to rise, expand, and express love, compassion, and empathy. It's the outward flow of affection and care for others, much like the upward motion of the teeter-totter, lifting and elevating those on the other side.

The downward swing represents the heart's capacity to receive love, kindness, and support. It's the willingness to be vulnerable and accept the love offered by others, like the rising motion of the teeter-totter, allowing itself to be lifted and supported.

If a teeter-totter becomes stuck in one position, it ceases to be fun or functional. Similarly, if the heart becomes imbalanced—either giving too much without reciprocity or closing itself off to receiving—it can lead to emotional strain and hurt.

A healthy heart, like a balanced teeter-totter, finds joy and fulfillment in the continuous exchange of love. It understands that giving and receiving are interconnected, each dependent on the other for a fulfilling and meaningful experience.

> Polarity, or action and reaction, we meet in every
> part of nature; in darkness and light; in heat and

cold; in the ebb and flow of waters; in male and
female; in the inspiration and expiration of plants
and animals; . . . Whilst the world is thus dual, so
is every one of its parts. The entire system of
things gets represented in every particle . . .

Ralph Waldo Emerson

BEFORE WE CAN GRASP NON-DUALITY

It's difficult to truly grasp the essence of non-duality, because we must first understand the nature of duality. Duality arises when we categorize emotions, thoughts, and experiences as opposites—love versus hate, good versus bad, us versus them. Separation perpetuates judgment, limited understanding, and the illusion of a fragmented and conflicted world. In our everyday perception, duality dominates our understanding of the world. We superimpose dualistic thoughts and emotions onto our experience, creating unnecessary suffering.

Non-duality, on the other hand, offers an understanding and experience beyond opposition. It allows us to see reality as a whole. Non-dual awareness fuels new actions in the world. It is a force, a revolutionary act, a radical shift from the narrow confines of self-centeredness. We understand that what we believe is true or right may, in fact, be only a view.

Non-duality empowers us to engage in acts of kindness not out of a sense of duty or obligation, but as an expression of our interconnectedness with all beings. It's an understanding that responsibility arises from a feeling of connection and belonging, that when we are not connected or don't feel connected, we quickly don't feel responsible. When the heartfelt sense of being connected is lacking, the fuel for kindness often rests on ego needs, hopes and fears of approval and disapproval, social expectations, rules, and habits. It takes two playmates to balance on the teeter-totter, agreeing to be in relationship, not jumping off and leaving the other to crash to the ground.

WHEN SELF-CARE BECOMES ALL-BEING CARE

Non-dual compassion recognizes that true self-care involves nurturing oneself not as an end but as a means—a means for cultivating the inner resources necessary to extend compassion to others. It's akin to filling one's cup with the intention of sharing the overflow with those around us.

In my childhood, care of others was emphasized, and care of self was minimized. It was a "you count, I don't count" equation. It was a central message in the religious patriarchy I grew up in. Self-care was minimized too quickly, and self-absorption was branded. And, of course, it could be that self-absorption was intended as an antidote to that potential threat of the patriarchy.

Only in adulthood did I understand the essentialness of self-care and the value of self-counting. Clients were often my teachers. As I worked with religious sisters, women who had joined the order at a young age, I saw how my imprinting mirrored theirs. I, too, had been taught that to love meant emptying myself (to the point of martyrdom) for others.

As one of the ordained sisters opined, "It feels heretical to count myself. Like a heresy!"

Nowadays, my view has changed. In terms of the self-care that was lacking in my early teachings, I see a swing to the opposite excess—an overweighting toward self-care, to self-indulgence at the expense of care for others.

I think again of the teeter-totter stuck with one side up or one side down. For me, caring needs to reflect the state of harmony of a teeter-totter swinging up *and* down, moving in balance for both parties.

Swinging upward is to rise in the current of love's energy, the flow of affection and care. To be held up and elevated like the wind under a bird's wing.

The descending swing is the heart's capacity to bow, as well as to carry the weight of care, the paradoxical tension of strength in vulnerability. The descent is a release into an emptiness that allows and prompts the heart's inhale, which, like the out-breath, is the doorway to rebirth and renewal of continuity.

When we balance our physical, emotional, and spiritual self-care needs, we become better equipped to serve others authentically and sustainably, transforming our individual pursuits into a collective endeavor of caring for all beings.

WHOLENESS AND INDIVIDUALISM: BOTH/AND

True self-care happens when we embrace the interplay between individualism and wholeness, not as a dichotomy but as an unbounded, dynamic force. A continuous process of self-discovery and integration within the wholeness of continuity. When we can assert our individuality while honoring our interconnectedness—both/and—a deep sense of purpose and harmony arises.

It's tempting to think of individualism and wholeness as distinctly different constructions, and thus to quantify, congeal, and freeze them into polarized opposites. I pull a tray of ice cubes (once water) from my freezer. I drop cubes into my glass. The quality of "flow" renders itself easy to control and handle in its present appearance of solid form! Only when the "solid" formations shapeshift back into their fluid state do I directly experience the dynamic dance of flow again. Now, it is less concretely available to my desire to isolate for easy management.

Individualizing, the process of becoming distinct from others, is essential to personal growth. It enables us to explore and develop our unique identity, values, beliefs, and aspirations. As individuals, we embark on self-discovery from the earliest stages of life—carving out our place in the world, asserting autonomy, and defining our boundaries and preferences.

However, alongside the pursuit of individuality lies an innate yearning for the wholeness of belonging—a longing to feel connected and integrated, to know ourselves and be known as part of something greater than oneself. This desire for wholeness in community manifests in various forms: a yearning for meaningful connections with others, a search for purpose and fulfillment, or a quest for spiritual or existential alignment.

If the search for individualism is the beginning of the journey, the achievement of interrelated connectedness—of being valued as part of the whole—is the completion. And yet it is not a one-time sequential journey, but a continuing dance.

Whereas the ego ideal of perfection, with its unattainable standards, encourages us to deny and hide our flaws, the loving embrace of community provides a container for unveiled self-acceptance.

In identification with others, we stand known and unveiled. In the humility of acceptance of our shared common humanity, we learn to accept our "brokenness as an integral part of life," as Parker J. Palmer says. We open ourselves up to growth, healing, and a deeper engagement with others, paving the way for authentic wholeness.

> Wholeness does not mean perfection: it means
> embracing brokenness as an integral part of life.

Parker J. Palmer

TIME ALCHEMIZES OUR ENEMIES

In chapter 10, I briefly mentioned the years I lived in Munich with my then-husband, a physicist invited to do his post-doctoral work at the Max Planck Institute. Today, my years there still puzzle me. It was only 20 years after the liberation from Nazi occupation in Holland. I still remember the days when the troops left—the jubilation, the *rusks* with orange sprinkles, the orange banners, the dancing in the streets, the joy in my siblings' faces.

I remember my father's response when I told him we were going to Munich. He flared up in anger and said, "Go to Moscow, not Munich." To me, going to Munich seemed exciting. The war did not overshadow my curiosity. It didn't seem like such a big deal, but now, in my eighties, I find myself trying to recall what I was thinking.

Today, I think of Munich as the city where Hitler's power consolidated, the foundation of the Nazi movement. I think of the Beer Hall Putsch (Hitler's failed coup d'état in 1923) and Dachau, the first concentration camp established in 1933.

Sixty years filter my memory. A summer trip to Berchtesgaden and Obersalzberg, his "Eagle's Nest." I worked in an American army library outside of Dachau. I read *Sueddeutsche Zeitung* daily, the Munich newspaper, with its editorials on Bavarian self-reflection and cultural analysis asking, "How could we have done this?"

Reminders of war were everywhere: rubble still on many streets. I saw men and women who had lived in

Nazi times. What I remember today of living in Bavaria is that I saw my neighbors then primarily as neighbors. Perhaps I had been too young for the branding still so fresh in my father's life to keep its hold. Maybe for me, the categories that had been so entrenched for my father had been lifted as circumstances changed and disappeared from daily experience.

I don't remember wanting to or even considering engaging in serious discussion about the war with anyone at the Max Planck Institute. I remember private curiosity, wondering, "Where were you? What were you doing?" As I interacted with adults my father's age, I do not remember hostility. I remember no mention of the war at all.

Since my husband and his family had lived in the United States and his father had not served or been directly involved in the war, perhaps he had little curiosity. His passion for physics and being in sync with the elite assortment of physicists and scientists at the Institute may have been all-consuming. Perhaps because I was a very young woman, I was intimidated; keenly aware of my relative ignorance in the face of their superior cultural sophistication, it may have seemed too far out of my league. When not working, we did all we could to take in culture. I know I was "star-struck." I recall that at one party I "touched" five Nobel Prize winners, privately and surreptitiously collecting those stolen touches as trophies!

As I write this, I remember an incident in Minnesota from 10 years ago. I was in a local Vietnamese restaurant with a friend who had been a helicopter gunner in Vietnam. He had sent me pictures of himself armed with his weapon in the doorway of a Chinook. The young waitress, born in America, did not flinch when he said he had been in 'Nam. She said, "I hope you will visit in peacetime; it's beautiful."

FOES CAN BE CATALYSTS FOR SELF-REFLECTION

At first glance, the idea of foes contributing to our well-being appears antithetical to personal growth. After all, the fact of "us versus them" is ingrained in our evolutionary human view. We know foes as those who disrupt, challenge, and sometimes inflict deep wounds on our tender psyche. They are sources of stress; they create friction, dissent, and sometimes discord. A demonized view of foes, especially in a context of war for survival, serves us in seeing them as different, as other, as "not us." That branding is permissive and allows us to subjugate, use, and even destroy them.

I think of how we destroy each other with gossip. The many ways we dehumanize the other and use that dehumanization as permission to commit morally injurious acts of violence, aggression, and inhuman cruelty on each other with impunity.

My friend who fought in Vietnam speaks to me of moral injuries. He speaks of his conscience, of having stepped outside the line of his own moral values. His willingness to transgress was triggered by seeing "the enemy," the Viet Cong, in a small village and raining napalm on the land.

Yet, delve deeper, and the significance of our foes becomes apparent. In their antagonism lies a profound paradox—foes can be catalysts for self-reflection, prompting us to confront our weaknesses, and bring parts of ourselves that might otherwise lay dormant to light, either positive or negative. For instance, although he has never spoken of it, I know my father took the life of others. Some capacity in him was called out in war, revealed, that might never otherwise have been actualized.

Though uncomfortable and often challenging, the presence of those we designate as foes in our lives can be a source of enrichment if we are self-reflective. Engagement can be a catalyst for self-discovery, resilience, and personal growth.

Think back to how my mother and I gave water to the retreating soldiers, after her initial vehemence not to do so. Instead, she saw how "the enemy" was also just a thirsty child who had been conscripted into war. We are so quick to assign negative valence to people who are different and so fast to see the difference as dangerous or wrong. We know from history that if we are exposed to each other, those marked differences lose their signal significance as "enemy" or "potentially dangerous."

Foes are not, need not, be morally repugnant presences. They can be opposing principles or behaviors. They can be new experiences that first feel alien, that trigger opposition. We all have certain personality qualities or tendencies in varying degrees: to be fearful, to want control, to be creative, to enjoy resting in comfort, to be eager to explore. Things congruent for one of us may be unwanted "foreignness" to someone else. Individual qualities can be excessive and out of balance, such as being highly anxious, quickly startled, and aroused. Alternately, another may be fast or slow to anger. Sometimes, we amplify (exaggerate) qualities and traits and expect others to share or comply with our preferences.

We can experience "foes" within our families when personalities and life experiences are so different. In my role as a family therapist, I often witnessed how a fearful, anxious parent would come into my office with a seemingly fearless offspring; how "hovering" parental control triggered rebellion; and how parents who saw their children as narcissistic extensions often ended up in a relationship with counter-dependent offspring. I have seen teenagers trying to soothe anxious parents, as well as teenagers who angrily took great rebellious risks to prove an anxious parent wrong. To confirm that not every venture was life threatening or fraught with peril and danger.

The presence of otherness represented as foes can provide a litmus test for the authenticity and strength of our convictions. Dissenting opinions force us to reconsider our valued opinions, long-held beliefs, and behaviors toward others. Their actions, motivations, and perspectives often serve as a stark reflection of our own fears, insecurities, or unacknowledged desires. By confronting these shadows within, we unravel layers of self-deception and attain a deeper understanding of our own complexities.

Life challenges temper us and change us. Adaptation instills tenacity. Duality of us versus them becomes non-dual compassion. As we hold the tension and continue our journey, once-enemies become friends, wounds become sinews of strength and character, and painful self-discovery transmutes chaos into wisdom.

MY WELL-BEING DEPENDS ON YOUR WELL-BEING

Feed the child, and you are feeding yourself.
Let her go hungry, and you too go hungry. Are
you going to sit around debating whether or
not the starving child really exists? Are you
going to give her a little bit of your bread?

Jeff Foster

Before we lived in Munich for his postdoctoral work, my then-husband accepted a fellowship from Ohio University for his PhD in high-energy physics. We packed up and moved to Athens, close to the West Virginia border. In the barracks of student housing, I befriended a neighbor, the wife of another graduate student, who taught in the Appalachian village of Glouster, 15 miles north of Athens. Knowing I was searching for something to do, she told me the school was being offered money to create something new, a special education program. And they were looking for a teacher. "Why don't you apply?" she asked.

I didn't think I had a chance. With a major in English literature, a minor in philosophy, and no education credits, how would I even qualify?

"What do you have to lose?" my friend said.

So, I made a call.

The superintendent came to the barracks to meet me. I had been painting; the not-yet-dry canvases hung on the wall. He asked if I had painted them. When I said yes, he said, "That will work," and he gave me the job.

In the coming months, I also got an education—of a different sort. My life had prepared me for hardship: the Occupation and immigration to Canada at eight years old. I remembered seeing an article about the grim reality of Appalachia's coal-mining poverty in *LIFE* magazine in 1959.[25] I had found a part of the United States that lived in a poverty that matched the years of war. I knew Appalachia was poor, but given my past, I thought I could relate to it. I could and did, but it broke my heart.

The kids in my class were the poorest of the poor. Three kids from one family took turns coming to school because they had only one pair of shoes. That wasn't the worst of it. I discovered that a 12-year-old girl was being trafficked for money by her own family.

---

25 "A Grim Instance in Coal Country," *LIFE*, April 13, 1959, https://books.google.com/books?id=VkgEAAAAMBAJ&lpg=PP1&pg=PA34#v=twopage&q&f=false.

In the two years that I worked at the Glouster school, I taught myself about special education. I sought support from the State Department of Education in Columbus, the capital of Ohio. Although I had no background in education, because my husband was a student at Athens University, I consulted with professors in the university's education department. With the help of a church where I was teaching Sunday school and the assistance of those professors, I started a food and clothing drive.

I discovered that the kids in my room had not been tested but selected for my class by virtue of being "misfits." It soon became clear to me that the materials I had been allocated for the purpose were unwanted and outdated teaching materials from other classrooms. When I discovered that the superintendent was using the special education money for different programs, I called the Columbus Board of Education representatives. I triggered an investigation and a change in program and staffing. It was my first venture into activism.

In the decades since, my mind often goes back to those kids whom I loved. Kids who needed so much and received so little. Kids who were being controlled and punished by a thick wooden paddle hanging near the blackboard in every classroom. I remember being forced to watch when Elijah, one of the kids in my room, was paddled. Today I wish I had objected. At the time, I did not yet understand that I might have exercised that action.

To this day, the faces of those children remain with me, as do the memories of life together in the classroom. Singing "Puff the Magic Dragon." Ted's flying squirrel roaming on desks, hiding in his shirt pocket. Annie sitting in the crook of my arm at her desk. Long nights in the barracks preparing individual lesson plans for each kid, since all were at different levels of proficiency.

What did I learn from those two years? I learned that my well-being depends on their well-being. I learned that no matter how full my belly is, I will always be hungry. I taught kids how to make pots of lentil and bean soup in the kitchen of the home economics department. We planted a garden that they harvested when school was out in the summer. We took excursions to local stores, teaching them how to shop for food that could be stored and made into soup. I taught them values and self-care and assured them of their human dignity and values. It was all I could do. I wish it could have been more.

We are all bound together in a dance of interbeing where every thought, action, and word ripples through the interconnected web. When we pause to reflect on this inter-dependence, a profound shift occurs within us.

> If you have come here to help me you are
> wasting your time, but if you have come
> because your liberation is bound up with
> mine, then let us work together.
>
> *Aboriginal activists group, Queensland, 1970s* [26]

SURVIVAL OF THE KINDEST

Although Charles Darwin is most associated with the term "survival of the fittest," he did not coin the phrase, nor did he intend for it to be used to justify the unrestrained competition of cutthroat capitalism or the assertion that "might

———

26 Aboriginal activist, artist, and academic Lilla Watson has been cited as this quote's source but because her words arose from a collective process, she wanted them to be credited as "Aboriginal activists group, Queensland, 1970s. https://lillanetwork.wordpress.com/about/.

is right." In fact, Darwin's conclusions were far more encompassing and inclusive than the concept of survival of the fittest, for which he is known.

Fortunately, most modern biologists reject the phrase "survival of the fittest." Christopher Kukk, author of *The Compassionate Achiever,* offers more insight, suggesting that "survival of the kindest" more appropriately captures Darwin's theory of natural selection. Kukk asserts, "The bumper-sticker way of teaching and labeling Darwin's ideas as exclusively focused on the 'survival of the fittest' is not only misleading; it completely misses his idea that humanity's success hinges on its level of compassion or sympathy."[27]

One of the most important yet overlooked aspects of Darwin's theories is his recognition of other qualities that contribute to well-being and survival. In 1871 in *The Descent of Man,* Darwin wrote that communities with the most sympathetic members were more likely to flourish. The capacity to act with empathy, sympathy, or concern for others can be seen in animals, even across species. Darwin argues that this capacity in humans—such as to risk yourself by jumping in a river to save another, as one dramatic example—comes from more than instinct or a momentary impulse:

> To do good in return for evil, to love your
> enemy, is a height of morality to which it may be
> doubted whether the social instincts would, by
> themselves, have ever led us. It is necessary that
> these instincts, together with sympathy, should

---

27 Christopher L. Kukk, *The Compassionate Achiever: How Helping Others Fuels Success* (New York: HarperCollins, 2017).

have been highly cultivated and extended by the aid of reason, instruction, and the love or fear of God, before any such golden rule would ever be thought of and obeyed.[28]

Darwin was pointing out the importance of habit, practice, discernment, even the power of communal values and accountability, that lead to a collective valuing of kindness—and even acting with kindness. Darwin named courage as well: "Nevertheless many a civilized man, or even boy, who never before risked his life for another, but full of courage and sympathy, thus disregarded the instinct of self-preservation, and plunged at once into a torrent to save a drowning man, though a stranger." And, as we've discussed, courage comes from the heart.

LISTEN TO YOUR HEART

The heart's voice, of course, is a metaphor.

When we say "Listen to your heart," we assume that the heart speaks in resonance with our inner moral compass and our capacity for empathy.

Josef Herschel was born in a Jewish family in World War II. In a YouTube interview, he tells the poignant story of how his parents, realizing they were about to be killed, entrusted him to the care of strangers. He marvels at the immensity of that choice, the cost to them of giving him away rather

---

28 Charles Darwin, The Descent of Man and Selection in Relation to Sex (New York: D. Appleton, 1909), 108–114. https://www.google. com/books/edition/The_Descent_of_man_and_selection_in_rela /jnTUvf_qEs4C.

than keeping him with them as they boarded the trains. Now in his late eighties, he still grieves when he sees children bonded with their parents, that sense of belonging, of being together. "I never had that," he says.

He goes on to speak of listening to the heart and making choices from the heart. "I can't imagine what went through their heads, their eldest, first child," he says. "We have choices in life. So many things influence us, and every choice has at least two possibilities—left or right. So, what's the right direction? The right direction is what your heart tells you."[29]

That sounds good to me, and I want to agree, but something in me knows that it's not entirely on track; there is more to it than it fails to consider the complexity of the heart's life. Life is changing, and the heart, like everything else, is not one-size or one-time-fits-all. The heart evolves, changes, and transmutes with time and experience.

Here is what holds me up: We all begin, in a sense, self-centered. If all goes well, we grow up in developmental changes. Not all hearts change equally; not all hearts grow, evolve, and continue to transform and transcend earlier stages. If you think of a ladder of development, some climb higher, while some get stuck on lower rungs. A heart that doesn't evolve stays stuck, remaining focused on early levels marked by immediate personal needs (physical and ego) and desires. "What's in it for me?" is the dominant question for earlier rungs of development; caring is limited to those who are directly connected to us or serve us somehow. A young, undeveloped, "childish" heart can be housed in an

---

29 Tswi Josef Herschel, "'Whose Child Are You?' The Story of Tswi Josef Herschel," Yad Vashem, April 27, 2017, YouTube video, 16:20, https://youtu.be/jy1RZweXQF8?si=WKd58UMRLsoqvmnI&t=825.

aging body, sadly interrupted. If that heart could speak, it would continue to say things like "I want," "That's mine," "Don't touch, "I don't want to help," or "It's too risky; I'm too scared to do that."

If it continues to develop, the heart expands, now to conform, guided by the need to be a part of something bigger. To belong, it will ask, "What will others think?" Now care extends but remains restricted, limited to family, friends, and the community. When the heart chooses to help, it's often guided by rules like "That's what friends do." In early stages, the heart is quickly caught up in the busyness of life, distracted by external stimuli.

Only later can the heart move solidly beyond the rungs of the self and those who impact the self. Now, the heart cultivates a stronger sense of personal values and ethical principles. The question is more frequently, "Given what is happening, what is the most just and compassionate thing to do?" There is a broader inclusion: the heart now is activated by a sense that all deserve dignity, respect, and care, and the heart has integrated a new sense of responsibility: "I must stand up for what I believe in, even if it's unpopular." The heart now searches for meaning and purpose, wrestles with uncertainty, and asks deeper questions.

Of course, these levels aren't strictly linear, and we all simultaneously exhibit characteristics of multiple levels. Various factors influence our heart's development, including personal experience and cultural context.

Not long ago, I received a call. My friend Tom was back in the hospital; in fact, he was in the emergency room headed for surgery. Could someone come to be with him? My heart opened with concern. I knew what Tom was dealing with.

Three weeks earlier, I had sat with him and waited. That day, I called the police to request that they go to Tom's daughter's apartment for a wellness check. The police had called back to tell us that they had found his daughter dead on the floor.

Tom has been a friend for many years. He is now cognitively impaired. He was a Vietnam veteran, a war I had actively resisted. He had served in good faith. He felt the government had lied to him as a young man wanting to serve his country. Because soldiers had saved my life, I had committed to stand by him if he needed help.

It was evening. I had flown home that morning after visiting my sister. I had settled in for the night, relieved to have a quiet evening after days of traveling, home again with my cat. After fixing a quick meal, I was tired, and my introversion was pleading for downtime.

As I listened to the phone call about helping Tom, I needed to make a choice. To go or stay at home.

The internal wrestling began.

Should I stay or go? I was as close to family as Tom had. His only brother was in Florida. His daughter was gone. I sat back and took a few breaths. I wanted to let myself off the hook.

I thought of what my friends might say: *You are old; it's okay not to go; someone else will appear. You are tired, and you deserve to rest. You can't do it all, and you can't take care of everyone. He is in the hospital; they will take care of him. You count, too.*

I could hear the other side: *You are closer to him than anyone else, and he feels safe with you. This has got to be frightening and overwhelming for him. I don't want him to be alone. You can rest tomorrow.*

Both choices would have consequences. If I went, I would not have the opportunity to rest as I had longed for. I would need to get dressed again, and I would have to drive in the dark. Or I could take the chance that he would be alone in the ER. I would have to live with not having his back when he needed someone. I would need to put my fatigue and longing to rest ahead of his urgent situation.

I could feel the decision rising in me. I had to go. It was the right thing.

I went. He smiled when I arrived at 8:30 p.m. While we sat in his dark room, I held his hand and played soft chants on his phone. I advocated for him, asked for water, and helped him to swallow. For hours, the testing equipment was wheeled in and out. Lines were inserted into his arm. He finally left for surgery at 1:15 a.m.

I was glad I went. I had done what felt like the right thing. I was very tired, so I canceled a meeting the next day.

AWAKENING COMPASSION

Our emotions deeply influence our hearts. Brené Brown eloquently writes that courage isn't vulnerability minus fear; it's vulnerability plus fear. As our hearts develop, something important happens: we become more willing to embrace vulnerability and take risks, even to sacrifice, *for what we believe in*. Courage may even bestow a warrior-like fierceness that allows us to navigate through our fear and discomfort.

A Dutch Catholic priest and writer, Henri Nouwen, speaks of emotional ripening, the journey from loneliness to solitude. He writes how the heart expands variously in its capacity for love and connection. He describes how the divided heart, longing for connection but caught between the desire for love and the fear of vulnerability, builds walls to protect itself from pain. He reveals how the wounded, hardened heart must fight ferociously if it is ever to open to trust, forgiveness, and authentic connection to others.

He suggests that the heart's compassion awakens when we finally accept our brokenness and the brokenness of the world.

Our heart journeys differ. We seem to all begin with naivete, a time when our hearts judge easily and see the world in simple terms; the young, naïve heart sees only easy choices and clear distinctions between good and evil. If we travel, our hearts see more deeply, life and its choices become complex, and the earlier simplicity is "broken open." As our naïve illusions shatter, as we experience loss, failure, injustice, and betrayal, something new arises from the ashes.

Wise elders promise that if we continue, we may be born into a deeper knowing, even the mystical discovery of the interconnectedness of all things. This awakening is often described in sacred texts as overflowing with love, seeing the divine in everyone and everything.

Each heart journey and each heart voice are unique. However, there is common agreement that their evolution is a lifelong process involving joy and sorrow, challenge and growth, and the arrow of upward progression always points in the direction of greater love, inclusion, compassion, and understanding.

> If I am not for myself, who will be for me? And if I am only for myself, then who am I? And if not now, when?
>
> *Rabbi Hillel*

Heart Questions

1. When is a time you felt connected to the unity of all life while still honoring the uniqueness of your personal experience and perspectives?

2. Who or what has been a "foe" in your life, and what did you learn about yourself—gifts or challenges—from your connection?

3. How does the concept of interconnectedness inform your understanding of compassion, recognizing that separateness is an illusion?

Chapter 12

Entering the Cave of the Heart

You are not a drop in the ocean. You
are the entire ocean in a drop.

Rumi

———

WHEN WE WERE fresh out of the womb, life was an oceanic orchestra of undifferentiated sights, sounds, and sensations. No inner/outer, self/other, psyche/soma, or distinction between mother, warmth, and nourishment. Mother was the being-state of warmth and nourishment. A wet diaper, on the other hand, was pure, unadulterated grief.

In her book *The Grace in Dying*, Kathleen Singh talks about three stages of development that reflect different positions in the self's unfolding interaction with Life. The first stage is the oceanic self, the undifferentiated self. The second, which arises after birth, is the unfolding of a separate ego-self. The third is transpersonal. According to Singh, progressing from pre-personal to personal to transpersonal is the natural unfolding of a human consciousness.

Some people, demoralized and discouraged by the problems of our times, idealize the past and hope to return to a state of oceanic bliss or the Garden of Eden. For me, the path moves forward, not back, to ongoing unfolding and transcending, into an ever deeper understanding of the mystery of being and life itself.

In this chapter, we're entering the cave of the heart, a place of mystery and paradox. The cave of the heart is the birthplace of questions that really matter, that stir the psyche, mystify and inspire, confound and perplex rational thought.

In this chapter, we're asking the biggest question of all: *Who are we?*

CAVE DIVING

From an early age, I was drawn to water. It may be because much of Holland, including the area where I was born, is reclaimed land held in place by dikes.

My mother was terrified of water. Her sister's child had drowned. For the rest of my mother's life, she would compare all bad things to the horror of a child drowning. If I ventured near the stream that flowed at the edge of our property, she would hover nearby with constant warnings to be careful. If I was disappointed or otherwise upset, she would remind me that "it wasn't a child drowned." Maybe that was why, although I was a teenage summer lifeguard in a two-foot-deep playground pool, I had never really become a good swimmer.

But the sea fascinated me, and the 10-day trip across the ocean as an emigrating child imprinted a sense of its mystery in me. Scuba diving let me swim in that mystery up close, despite my initial claustrophobia.

It must have been 100 dives before I could descend free of fear. Breathing underwater is not natural for humans. I knew it, and my body knew it. It took many dives before I trusted my gear and developed enough confidence to breathe easily, to hover in "full lotus," neutrally buoyant and suspended in water as naturally as the fish around me. Those were ecstatic moments when I felt overwhelmed with gratitude and wonder to have access to that otherwise strange, inaccessible world. (When I read that the military might be trying to find a way to create a solution that divers could inhale that would allow them to dive without tanks, I felt ready to sign up.)

In Frank Herbert's science fiction novel *Dune,* the hero practices an ancient mantra, "The Litany Against Fear."

> Fear is the mind-killer. Fear is the little-death . . .
> I will permit it to pass over me and through me.
> And when it has gone past, I will turn the inner
> eye to see its path. Where it the fear has gone
> there will be nothing. Only I will remain.[30]

As I mentioned in chapter 8, this mantra has been my personal litany that always calms me down. During one dive with my friend Ted, it may just have saved my life.

Ted and I were cave diving at a depth of about 100 feet on a beautiful day with good visibility and plenty of light. The opening to the cave we were visiting was about the size of a regular doorway. We entered the cave, unaware that other divers were behind us. Suddenly the visibility in the cave became darkly opaque. A small group of inexperienced divers had come in and stirred up silt with their fins while attempting to balance on the cave floor. The entrance to the relatively small cave was suddenly darkened and crowded. My claustrophobia was triggered. I panicked, could not breathe. In the cloudy darkness, Ted was not available for the support a dive buddy would typically provide in a panic situation. It was beyond uncomfortable. It was terrifying.

———

30 Frank Herbert, *Dune,* 16th ed. (New York: Berkley Books, 1980).

I began the familiar ritual: *Fear is the mind killer, fear is the little-death, I will let it flow through me.* I started to breathe through the panic. It took many breaths. Paradoxically, I "forced" relaxation by focusing on and regulating my breath against my body's instinct. As waves of terror washed over me, I concentrated on the sound of my breath until it became smooth and even. I touched and felt the hardness of the cave wall, leaned my hand out against it, allowed its solidity to anchor me. Hovering against the wall, finding specks of visibility and shielded by the continuous thread of the litany, I continued to breathe until the fear lifted and quietness returned. Afterward, I could feel the adrenaline in my body surge for several hours, but I had continued to breathe. I had allowed my fear to flow through me. And I had survived. I felt exaltation.

"Why would you do that?" my sister asked a month later when I told her the story.

"Because I can," I replied, not expecting Nelly to understand.

We all have places in our hearts that live behind closed doors. There are caves in the heart that test us and threaten the ego. In his book *The Denial of Death*, Ernest Becker writes that our fear surrounding our ego's survival matches our fear of death. Voluntary entrance into these darkened places is a kind of laboring; exposure to what is hidden comes with feelings of risk and danger—the entry into loss of control and surrender to an unknown that feels dangerous. Voluntary exploration of that cave requires courage and a willingness to take risks. Reframing of the ego and alterations in our projected self-image can feel like death, and yet, the humbling deconstruction of these idealized images can, when faced and held in the generosity of compassion and allowed to run their course, expand our capacity for the gifts of life—a hard birthing that can awaken undreamed-of potential.

Years later, I remembered that cave-diving day as a mother in my office listened to her daughter describe sexual abuse by her stepfather, her mother's husband. I saw the mother shudder, her body trembling as if grasping for air. "Do you think I could've known?" she shouted at her daughter.

"I don't know how you could *not* have known, Mom," her daughter said.

The realization came again with another client. It was an autumn day—the room was growing dark, and I had just turned on the light. It was the last session of the day, and I was listening to a businessman, an older adult whose marriage was floundering. His wife, also a psychologist, gave him my name when she learned of my childhood during World War II. "She thought I should tell you; that you might understand," he had said when introducing himself. There had been a long moment of silence. I could see the color in his face changing, a shuddering inhale. He gathered himself. Then told a story.

Back when he was only a few weeks out of his teens, he had been called up from the reserves to serve in the Korean War. He looked at his hands, then glanced quickly at me. "Can you handle this?" he asked.

I countered, "Yes. Have you ever told anyone this story?"

He shook his head. We sat quietly together, making eye contact. I met his gaze as he leaned in. He had been not yet a man, shipped to hell in northern Korea.

"Three days later," he continued, now in a steely-edged voice, "I became a weapon of death by bayonet." There was a sharp inhale, a release. He squeezed out the words, spoke of the sound, smell, and sight of ripping flesh revealed through the shreds of a torn uniform. He paused.

"Afterwards, I went to talk with the parent of a lad who had been deployed with me. I brought them false news about how he had died. I wanted to bring comfort, not heartache."

That afternoon, we sat quietly together into the evening. Now and again, he wept. When he reached out, I met his eyes and held his hand. I remembered the war. I knew something of those who live with moral injury.

He had carried these memories alone until he found a support group for soldiers at the VA. Finally, he was able to integrate the memory he had opened. He found a band of brothers. The bonds of his marriage deepened in a new resilience.

Years later, I read of students caught in a cave in Thailand and of divers who, with the help of an anesthesiologist, found a way to get the kids out. I learned how ketamine had been used to subdue the natural terror of breathing underwater and how, "knocked out of consciousness," the children had been guided to safety with the skillful means of cave divers.

I thought again of cave diving as a metaphor for daring to explore the hidden places in the heart.

Spelunking is not safe. It requires training. One Thai rescue diver had died. The journey of cave diving to the heart is also not without danger.

Yet danger is often linked with opportunity. Entry can mean entry to greater understanding. Skill can be cultivated. Just as the power and resolution of technologies (microscopes, telescopes, and MRIs) can grant deeper penetration and understanding of veiled experience, entering the hidden caves of the heart can enliven us and provide a rebirth of understanding. The heart, too, can be explored.

It comes with risk—acceptance of danger. We have different paths. Some of us are called to stay with and cultivate the known and readily visible. We bring experience and gifts and do our work and live our lives outside caves. Others are called to enter grottos with only a partial view, while others become spelunkers. Heart divers, at times, can assist and rescue those suddenly below their familiar depths.

> Water is water, no matter what.
> The solidity of ice imagines itself to be
> edges and density. Melting, it remembers;
> evaporating, it ascends.
>
> *Stephen Levine*

TWO BECOME ONE

Once there lived a boy made of salt who wanted to know where he came from. So, he set out on a long journey that led him across snow-peaked mountains and wind-blown plains. Along the way, he questioned everyone he met. But no one could answer his burning question.

Finally, his long journey took him to the shore of the great ocean. It was the most magnificent thing he had ever seen. Entranced by sight and sound and smell, he was drawn ever closer to the waves lapping the shore.

As the sea roared to and fro, foaming and bubbling, it seemed to whisper his name in a strange and wordless way.

"How marvelous," he exclaimed.

Cautiously, he dipped his toe into the tide. The sea called to him from within and without, "If you wish to know who you are," it said, "you mustn't be afraid."

The salt boy took another step and felt the tide roll over his foot. "Ohhh!" he cried. Never had he experienced such joy! Exhilarated, he took another, then another, until he was running and splashing, going deeper and deeper—dissolving with each step—until there were no more questions, no more worries or concerns, no more mountains to climb or plains to cross.

"Ahhhh. Finally, I know who I am," he said, but now he spoke in the strange, wordless language of the great oceans.

The parable of the salt boy is very old (and sometimes told as the story of the salt doll). It's about this journey we are all on toward self-realization. A wave is not the ocean, and yet, it is not separate from the ocean. From birth, a wave is completely supported by the ocean—and at death, it is completely reabsorbed by the ocean. At no time is a wave separate from the ocean. At no time are we separate from the Universe.

Perhaps the reason the parable has been around for so long is that it helps us in two ways. First, it gives us a way to visualize the difficult mysticism of non-duality, of interdependence, or what the Vietnamese monk Thich Nhat Hanh called our *interbeing* nature.

Second, when you're feeling stuck, alone, and unsupported, the image of the salt boy uniting with the source of all life can initiate an alchemical reaction: a felt sense of connection to the entire universe. When your boundaries soften just a little, it can be a profoundly intimate experience. And possibly, some part of you will recognize the truth in it and respond in a deeply moving way.

When the salt boy entered the Great Ocean, two became one. Sacred teachings tell us that to enter the Heavenly Kingdom, we must let go of our limited, limiting ideas and beliefs. As we release, the doorway to new possibilities opens. Buddha taught that the nature of the universe is *not two/not one*. All great wisdom teachings say the same thing.

Just like the salt boy, we have both an individual and an undivided nature. And just like the salt boy, we all can experience our undividedness directly. It happens in an expansion of awareness that transforms experience. Rather than *hearing* a bird singing in a nearby tree, you *become* the bird, the song, and the tree. You don't *feel* the waves lapping at your feet; you *are* the waves, the salt, and the sand. You don't *see* a burning bush; you *are* the fire, and you are the bush. Absolute Wholeness, experienced in this way, is the essence of spiritual life.

> You will enter the Kingdom of Heaven
> when you make two one.
>
> *Jesus, the Gospel of Thomas*

THOU ART THAT

Here's another story you may be familiar with. It's from one of the world's earliest texts, the Upanishads. Like the story of the salt boy, it speaks to our need to feel that we belong and assures us that we can never actually be alone. The original tale is quite long, so this is just a passage from a much longer story.

Once, a very wise man was deeply concerned about his young son, who returned home full of pride after studying for 12 years with an eminent guru.

His father said, "Son, I know you have learned much. Please explain through what means do we hear the inaudible, perceive the unperceivable, and know the unknowable?"

"I am not aware of such knowledge, Father."

After a long moment, the father began to speak. "The rivers in the east flow eastward, the rivers in the west flow westward, and all enter the seas," he began. "From sea to sea, they pass, the clouds lifting them to the sky in vapor and then sending them down as rain. When rivers unite with the sea, they do not know whether they are this river or that.

"Just so, my son—be it lion, tiger, boar, or man—all beings lose their identities on returning to the Source. Indeed, all that exists is projected from the Subtle Essence, which pervades all and is the source of all. *That* is Reality. *That* is Self.

"And Thou art That, my son."

SEEING WITH BOTH EYES

There is in all visible things an invisible
fecundity, a dimmed light, a meek
namelessness, a hidden wholeness.

Thomas Merton

From a scientific perspective, we do not experience reality as it is.

One of my best lessons came when I was an intern. I was fortunate to have a brilliant, wise psychologist from the University of Chicago as a teacher. One day, I brought a client story to a weekly case consultation. He noticed that I was emphasizing the negative qualities of that client. He interrupted and asked me to place one hand over one eye and tell him what I could see. Then, to do the same with the other eye. Then he told me to open both eyes. "What is the difference?" he asked. "What do you see?"

Of course, I quickly told him that I now had depth.

"Remember that," he said firmly. "You will never know anyone deeply if you can see them only one-dimensionally. Human beings are multifaceted. To know them, you need to use your capacity for binocular vision. Only then can you know them as much as it is possible to know them."

The lens we see through changes what we see. When we look through both eyes, we suddenly find depth. It is as if we are inside our heads, looking at the world through two windows. Other than real and proverbial "blind spots," our eyes generally offer an accurate view of what's out there in front of us.

The scientific view is more complicated. It sees our ears collecting vibrations that flow through the air, our nose and tongue collecting chemical signatures, and our skin responding to tactile signatures. That we see reality as consisting of separate entities is a delusion created by consciousness.

Experiments replicated in laboratories worldwide clearly show a mysterious intertwining between consciousness and the physical world. The double-slit experiment, for example, suggests that consciousness may somehow influence whether an electron will show up as a wave or particle. Modern science has shown that everything in the universe is connected in ways that confound the rational mind.

Sir James Jeans, the English physicist, mathematician, astronomer, and author of *The Mysterious Universe,* put it this way, "The world begins to look more like a great thought than a great machine."

The voice of modern science has offered a powerful endorsement to what mystics and wisdom teachers have been teaching for thousands of years. Throughout the ages, mystics have directly experienced this flow of myriad manifestations arising from Oneness, which seems to mirror what modern science calls a morphic field of potential. A mystical experience inspires us; it creates a sense of wonder that can have far-reaching benefits to our emotional, spiritual, and physical health.

These experiences of heightened awareness used to be rare. Over time, however, our capacity to perceive the undivided nature of reality seems to be increasing as more of us engage in some form of contemplative practice, whether we call it centering prayer, meditation, yoga, or just pausing momentarily to experience the awe and wonder of our interconnected universe.

> Forfeit your sense of awe, let your conceit
> diminish your ability to revere, and the
> universe becomes a marketplace for you.
>
> *Rabbi Abraham Heschel*

EVOLVING A QUANTUM WORLDVIEW

A modern understanding of the universe as an intelligent cosmos began in 1925 with a new formulation of quantum physics. Suddenly, matter and the laws of classical physics no longer offered our only view of reality—it was just a layer. Underlying it was a field of subtle energy with very mysterious and confounding characteristics.

David Bohm, one of the most significant theoretical physicists of the twentieth century, said in a dialogue with Renée Weber:

> Consciousness is much more of the implicate
> order than is matter . . . Yet at a deeper level

[matter and consciousness] are actually inseparable and interwoven, just as in the computer game the player and the screen are united by participation. In this view, mind and matter are two aspects of one whole and no more separable than are form and content. Deep down the consciousness of mankind is one. This is a virtual certainty because even in a vacuum, matter is one; and if we don't see this, it is because we are blinding ourselves to it.[31]

During my time in Munich in the 1960s, I had a front-row seat to conversations about quantum physics as it was coming into its stride. I often accompanied my then-husband to Geneva, where his experiments were conducted at the CERN accelerator. The new ideas frequently seemed like something a science fiction writer had dreamed up.

As I have touched on elsewhere, the years in Munich, living in Hitler's home base with Germans who had lived in the war, did much to deepen my understanding of war and its impact. It was a time when my worldview opened and expanded.

I then learned that quantum physics proposed that consciousness, rather than chemistry, may be foundational to reality and that everything in the universe is somehow linked in ways that defy our understanding of time and space. Later, when I became familiar with Bohm's work, I learned that he saw the universe as a coherent *whole* engaged in an unending process of unfoldment. It made me think of how

---

31 David Parrish, 2006. *Nothing I See Means Anything: Quantum Questions, Quantum Answers* (Boulder, Colorado: Sentient Publications, 2005). Also see Renée Weber, *Dialogues with Scientists and Sages: The Search for Unity* (London: Routledge & Kegan Paul, 1986).

Aristotle said, "The whole is greater than the sum of its parts." (Aristotle's words were later taken up by Gestalt therapy and often repeated in family systems theory). From time immemorial and across cultures, mystics who have touched the deepest levels teach that Ultimate Reality is unknown and unknowable—that it can't be explained or understood. The mystical nature of quantum physics brought up many questions with no clear answers, but its influence on physics and other disciplines was profound. It ushered in a new tolerance for the complexity of the universe.

> Science cannot solve the ultimate mystery of nature. And that is because, in the last analysis, we ourselves are part of nature and therefore part of the mystery that we are trying to solve.
>
> *Max Planck*

In quantum physics, our undivided nature is sometimes likened to a field of potential. If we can tap into this field of potential for just one moment, that will be a moment in which our individual worries, fears, and anxieties drop away. Even if it only lasts for a few moments, these mystical experiences can have far-reaching benefits; they alter what we "know" of reality in a way that can affect our emotional, spiritual, and physical health. How close can we actually come to our undivided nature? Well, how close is a wave to the ocean?

A hidden wholeness that is not separate from our consciousness assures us that while the unknowable cannot be understood—*it can be experienced.* And not only by the mystics—all of us have the capacity.

Zen teacher Norman Fischer once wrote in *Lion's Roar* about how humans depend on each other, that there could not be what we call a person without other people:

Literally every thought in our minds, every emotion that we feel, every word that comes out of our mouth, every material sustenance that we need to get through the day, comes through the kindness of and the interaction with others. And not only other people but nonhumans too, literally the whole of the earth, the soil, the sky, the trees, the air we breathe, the water we drink. We don't just depend on all of this; we are all of it and it is us.[32]

THE HEART'S INMOST REQUEST

Long ago in a faraway land, a king heard a sound he had never heard before. It was beautiful. He was drawn to it. The rising and falling of the sound lifted his spirit, opened his heart, and his soul soared.

But he couldn't see the source. So, he asked his attendants and one of them said, "It's the sound of a lute."

Immediately, the king exclaimed, "Bring me this lute." So, the lute was brought to him, and he began taking it apart, trying to find the beautiful music. Finally, when the lute was just a pile of wood, he cast it away and said, "Never mind the lute. Just bring me the music."

Hearing the music, the king awakened to something new, something he had never experienced or even imagined. It was as if a wall that he did not even know existed collapsed, and there before him was a vastness far beyond his understanding.

------

32 Norman Fischer, "Life is Tough. Here Are Six Ways to Deal With It," *Lion's Roar*, February 12, 2021, https://www.lionsroar.com/life-is-tough-six-ways-to-deal-with-it-march-2013/.

When the music stopped, all that he possessed no longer satisfied him. The music awakened him to his heart's deepest desire. In his own clumsy way, he sought to answer that inmost request of the heart. But what does a king, who is used to commanding the coarse, finite physical world with a word, know of the subtle, infinite Divine?

We are all searching for our deepest desire, our heart's inmost request. And in our own blundering way, we are each searching for the source of the proverbial music. In our own egocentric way, mixed with misplaced ideas of entitlement, we all know that life's music is our birthright. It is the melodious voice of our own heart. Being confused and knowing so little of a world beyond that perceived by our senses, we do not recognize our own true voice. We reject it, and having rejected it, embark on a journey to discover it.

> If we find ourselves with a desire that nothing
> in this world can satisfy, the most probable
> explanation is that we were made for another world.
>
> *C.S. Lewis*

THE END OF THE WORLD–AS WE KNOW IT

From a scientific viewpoint, the world we see more closely resembles a network of rivers, streams, and deltas than the separate, distinct entities our eyes see. Streams of electrical impulses, vibrations, and elemental particles/waves come together, interact for a while, and then move on.

Joseph Campbell, in a 1979 conversation with Eugene Kennedy for *The New York Times*, described the disconcerting shift that happened when astronauts stepped on the moon and television shared their first glimpse of our planet known as "earthrise." It up-ended the human view of a divided Heaven and Earth that also confirmed the separation, as Kennedy put it, of body and soul, nature and supernature, flesh and spirit. "With our view of earthrise," Campbell said, "we could see that the earth and heavens were no longer divided but that the earth is in the heavens." He goes on:

> The mystical theme of the space age is this: the world, as we know it, is coming to an end. The world as the center of the universe, the world divided from the heavens, the world bound by horizons in which love is reserved for members of the in-group: that is the world that is passing away. Apocalypse does not point to a fiery Armageddon but to the fact that our ignorance and our complacency are coming to an end.[33]

Science and mystics both have given us symbols to guide our journeys, both inner and outer. Joseph Campbell called earthrise one of those great symbols that acts as a compass. "One point is in a fixed place, but the other moves to the unknown. The fear of the unknown, this freefall into the future, can be detected all around us. But we live in the stars, and we are finally moved by awe to our greatest adventure. The Kingdom of God is within us."[34]

––––––––

33 Joseph Campbell, *Thou Art That: Transforming Religious Metaphor* (Novato, California: New World Library, 2001). See also Eugene Kennedy, "Earthrise: The Dawing of a New Spiritual Awareness," *The New York Times*, April 15, 1979, https://www.nytimes.com/1979/04/15/archives/earthrise-the-dawning-of-a-new-spiritual-awareness.html.

34 Campbell, *Thou Art That*, 114.

Throughout the ages, mystics have experienced this unfoldment of myriad manifestations arising from Oneness. Mystical experiences—direct contact with this field of potential—can have far-reaching benefits to our emotional, spiritual, and physical health. In Buddhism, direct contact with Oneness is called an enlightenment experience.

Whatever inspires you to follow a spiritual path—whether it's the parable of the salt boy, Buddha's teaching that the universe is "not one/not two," the teaching of Jesus that we must make two one, or the findings of modern science—in the end, all seem to point to the same inescapable conclusion: that we are thoroughly immersed in a profound and beautiful mystery. What's more—we *are* this profound and beautiful mystery.

> The most beautiful emotion we can experience is the mysterious. It is the source of all true art and science.
>
> *Albert Einstein*

HEART QUESTIONS

1. When have you had an experience where the boundaries between self and others seemed to soften? How did this experience manifest? As a momentary sense of awe or a deep realization of reality as it is, or something else?

2. What is your heart's inmost request or deepest desire? Did it arise from the cave of your own heart or from the firmly held beliefs of your parents or culture?

3. What's a situation where you might look "with both eyes" instead of only one?

Chapter 13

If the Heart Could Dream

Every great dream begins with a dreamer.
Always remember, you have within you the
strength, the patience, and the passion to
reach for the stars, to change the world.

Harriet Tubman

———

THROUGHOUT MY LIFE, I have witnessed and pondered how the doors of our heart-mind can open and close. I have met open, receptive, inquiring, even gullible hearts as well as hearts that seem guarded and locked down, impervious to change.

I was the first in my family to go to college (as I described in chapter 1). I had left Canada at 18 to pursue my education at a "church college" in Michigan. There, I was exposed to foreign students, roommates, professors, and many new and different, sometimes disturbing, values and ideas. Like many young people who leave home, I was confronted with change.

I returned to Canada on holiday break, eager to share my new insights. But on the first day, at a family coffee hour after church, I grew quiet, realizing that would not happen. Conversations were one-sided monologues. Family members pushed their way in, highlighting their achievements, and chit-chatting eagerly about daily events.

My thoughts and experiences, which I had been eager to share, were not invited. Efforts to share felt flat. I could not find a way for my changing self to have a voice and be included. I could participate, but only as a listener, keeping my new experiences out of the picture.

I felt disappointed and confused. I had been eager for mutual sharing and reciprocity. In time, a door slowly closed. I withdrew into an unshared inner journey, less keen to participate, no longer trying or hoping to share. My heart felt divided between the people I loved and the new truths transforming me into my own authentic self.

My ties to home grew thin. I rarely went back. When I did, conversations were limited to past experiences that had once served as a bridge. No longer in an immigrant-family echo chamber, I continued to expose myself to new ideas, stepping through new doors. I was listening to new voices. "Trying things on." I was ingesting, discarding, reviewing, and renewing my attitudes, beliefs, values, and identity. I was becoming who I was.

But I never stopped dreaming of a wider bridge allowing more traffic.

BUILDING BRIDGES

I was young then. It felt personal. Today, I see my family's reaction to "the new me" as a family-system dynamic and a universal relationship challenge. Systems resist change. But change is the nature of the river of life. Despite resistance to change, we are all caught up in the flow, and we all change—some more readily, some with more resistance. Change comes with risk. Change can separate and exact a cost, a "heart price." In my case (as for many who move away from a closed community), it was more than choosing to attend college in the U.S. It was not just the miles or geography. The unshared experiences had left an imprint on my heart. The cost was distance, a feeling of loss, loneliness, and separation.

Today, as I look at our society, I see the price of change. We are growing apart. As change occurs, we need more bridges, two-way bridges wide enough to sustain meaningful conversations. Neglect leaves us vulnerable and at risk. Opportunities for connection are lost when not constructed or cultivated. What happens at a family level can occur in a community or a country. We are living this scenario today; we saw it come to a desperate head in the U.S. election of November 2024.

Communication is the multi-colored span that can bridge our divides. Yet our conversations are a prism, constrained by habit, limited self-interest, discomfort with vulnerability. Acknowledged or hidden purpose and intention "drives the direction" of our path to connection.

There is a time for everything: chitchat, factual exchanges, ritualistic interactions, social engagement, self-disclosure, heart-full intimacy, and presence. Today, I see more clearly how each level serves different needs—building community, cultivating social participation, fostering personal growth, and strengthening relationships, each with its required skills and tools.

Unlike social conversations intended to be safe and comfortable, heart conversations—the bridging encounters that can transform, reach across divides—require courage, awareness, and an inclination for reciprocity. Profound connections that touch the heart and soul are demanding and have requirements. Above all, they need active listening and a genuine interest in "the other." Unfortunately, this capacity for connectedness is rare, something few of us have learned or are willing or able to extend.

If there was one sentiment I heard repeatedly in my decades as a therapist, it was, "They don't hear me; they don't see me; they don't know me." The remark that touched me most was when someone said, "I feel heard. I feel seen. I feel known."

Our world has many who talk and instruct. Fewer who listen. Yet intimate listening is the bridge that transcends surface encounters, that makes possible the profound connections that join hearts and souls. One way of standing between river and land is on the middle of a bridge where you can witness the water flowing below and the sun rise or set on the horizon.

THE MAGIC IS IN THE MIDDLE

We discover the true alchemy of connection in the middle of seeming opposites (polarized ideas, beliefs, choices). In the middle, we can offer our authenticity while honoring differences. In the middle, we make space for inner contradictions and vulnerabilities. Our humanity resides in the messy, imperfect middle.

Standing humbly in the middle, we find self-compassion. We acknowledge imperfection, that we are all works in process. That life is not fair, but we can strive to be fair.

That kind of magic manifests in proportion to our ability to navigate the middle ground between emotional suppression and excess. In the words of two book titles, it's the agony and the ecstasy found in the balance point of embracing full catastrophe living. That means allowing ourselves to feel our emotions fully and authentically without being overwhelmed or governed by them. It's a balancing dance where we cultivate emotional resilience and discover the capacity to respond to life's challenges with strength, sensitivity, and stability.

Often seen as contradictory or mutually exclusive, paradoxes show us how we can coexist harmoniously in this middle ground. Embracing paradoxes means accepting that things can be true *and* false, simple *and* complex, depending on the context. We can give ourselves permission to explore the spaces between certainties, knowing that the growth path involves navigating the gray areas of our complexity. And, in doing so, we can discover the beauty in the synthesis of opposites. There, instead of seeking a resolution, our focus shifts to *embracing the tension* between opposing concepts, allowing for a deeper understanding to emerge.

New perspectives often arise from the tension between what is and what could be. Middle ground provides the fertile soil where the seeds are planted and the magic of transformation takes root.

THE OPEN HEART OF PRESENCE

Our hearts' whispers and gentle nudging keep us on the path to wholeness and fulfillment, not found in the extremes but in the delicate balance that allows us to embrace the full spectrum of our shared humanity.

An undivided heart embodies a sense of unity—a state where thoughts, desires, and actions align harmoniously. It's where congruence between our inner values and outward expressions is unencumbered by conflicting motives, divided allegiances, or hidden agendas. It's where we can fully embrace the richness of our connections with others.

Our open, undivided heart allows us to become alchemists of our lives, to transform our everyday experiences into nuggets of wisdom, authenticity, and inner harmony. It reminds us that despite our diverse backgrounds, experiences, and perspectives, fundamental aspects of humanity unite us all.

One of my colleagues, a philosopher, once summarized an event by saying, "The wiser you feel, the dumber you may be." Shakespeare put it this way, "The fool doth think he is wise, while the wise man knows himself to be a fool." British philosopher Bertrand Russell said, "The whole problem with the world is that fools and fanatics are always so certain of themselves, and wiser people so full of doubts."

Scientists have explored this strange paradox. Two psychologists from Columbia University presented their research in a 1999 paper, which led to it being dubbed the Dunning-Kruger effect. This illusionary superiority came to be summed up as, "You don't know what you don't know."[35] They found that lesser-skilled individuals, not knowing how much they don't know, appear to overestimate their knowledge and ability. But this effect doesn't just happen to blatantly ignorant—it is a cognitive bias that can happen to any of us.

Paradoxically, those who dig more deeply are keenly aware of the vastness and complexity of life. When these individuals consider their knowledge of what they don't know, they conclude that they know very little. While the "deep divers" know how much more they must learn, surface swimmers are not deterred by that experience.

Thinking about thinking and knowing about knowing is what we know of as metacognition, an awareness of awareness. Metacognition allows us to "witness" and become aware of our thought processes, and to analyze and judge

---

35 Kat Boogaard, "The Dunning-Kruger Effect: Why and How We Overestimate Our Own Abilities," Work Life, Atlassian.com, https://www.atlassian.com/blog/productivity/dunning-kruger-effect.

our ideas, knowledge, and skills. This capacity seems to be difficult for those lacking this cognition.

Sadly, the less competent among us often rise to the top, carried by their sincere, delusional self-confidence. It's not just a problem in organizations, or leadership, but can also infiltrate the quality of our friendships and family ties.

> Real knowledge is knowing the
> extent of one's ignorance.
>
> *Confucius*

WHEN THE MIND CLOSES, THE HEART WAVERS

Years ago, I had a client I'll call John, an author and scientist who was also an immigrant from Central America. Weighted with bipolar depression, he told me his family story. It resonated with my immigrant experience. I think of it today in our divided country after the 2024 election.

"I grew up in a closed community. We were a minority. To preserve identity, we shielded ourselves carefully against outward influence. I came here for my education. I have changed. Now, when I return, I feel like an outsider. My siblings regard and love me dearly, but only from a well-maintained distance. They don't want to hear about or know how I have changed. The door to who I am now is firmly closed. Sometimes I feel they fear that my ideas are a toxin, a virus, that could infect them. I don't intend or want to influence them, but I wish I could share! It has not been easy; my understanding of life has been hard-earned. I know who I am. It would be so wonderful to be known!"

I asked John what remains. He replied, "Our historical sibling bond, our early familial love, *that* is still alive, but there are now caves in my mind and heart that will never be shared."

It was a sobering and familiar conversation. I knew John to be a self-aware, sincere man, a "Seeker." I knew of his willingness to meet the unknown, to grapple with complexity. John had wrestled hard with change, unlike those not called to deep inner work, those who created walls and fences in fear that the center would not hold against invasion. He had come to trust his inner capacity for discernment. His changes came from labor and a process of openness and curiosity, a yearning for truth transcending the limits of certainty.

John never experienced the "change of heart" he wished to see in his siblings. His family lived under political threat, and adaptation is not suited for times of physical danger.

But where possible, a change of heart requires an interest in what we don't already know.

Awareness is the antidote to the Dunning-Kruger effect. We can overcome it with curiosity, a willingness to listen, and the courage to open to change. It comes with confidence, a maturity that allows us to engage with paradox and ambiguity.

In some ways, John's story is everyone's story. As we mature, we are all offered the opportunity to "own" our core foundational beliefs, to weigh new values that life exposes us to and the values we take with us from the families and communities we grow up in.

We build and solidify the strength of that new foundation as we learn to trust our capacity for discernment. We are rewarded with freedom and confidence in safely navigating the inherent change and uncertainty in the river of life.

While this profound transformation was true for John, we are not all so able. For many, the heart remains closed, resistant to change. A hardened heart clings to an illusion of safety in orthodoxy, in the authority of custom, in the authority of the pre-ordained and familiar.

A hardened or closed heart is unwilling to change and unable to recognize that change could be good. It listens to authority. Fear of change often signals distrust in discernment, in our ability to sort new information against a central foundation of values. When trust in discernment is absent, difference becomes threatening. The heart remains closed to the river of change that is life. Fear of difference keeps the heart closed in seeming safety.

If the heart could dream, it might be willing to change. Open-mindedness leads to a change of heart. It can lead to love that lets us enter the caves of each other's hearts.

OPENING THE DOOR TO LISTENING

We each stand at the heart's door—the portal to knowing. We glance at the vast horizon, but do we truly *see* it with the astronaut's eyes, adrift in the cosmic silence? We note a blemish on our skin, yet can we grasp the intricate world the dermatologist unveils under her lens?

We hear a cry, a signal of distress, but do we all hear the same story? No. We each carry our own unique symphony of experiences, our own inner music that shapes how we perceive the world. What I glean from my vantage point, my relative position, may be vastly different from what you, or your child, or the stranger on the street experiences.

And so, how do we bridge this chasm of perception? How do we truly *know* another's inner world? It begins with a simple, yet profound question: *Do we really want to know?*

True knowing requires a willingness to *listen*—not passively, but with an active, engaged heart. It's a skill, a practice, a commitment to opening ourselves to the other. We must suspend our assumptions and our preconceptions to truly hear what is being said and what is left unspoken.

But let us be honest. We all have limits. But sometimes it's not about limits. Sometimes we don't truly want to listen. We prefer the comfort of our own familiar shores, the ease of our own perspectives. Surface knowing may serve us well, and we are content to leave knowing at a social glance, a fleeting connection, rather than feel the vulnerability of deep engagement. And, sometimes, those who want our ears are vampires, happy to meet their needs at our expense.

Active listening requires effort and a willingness to step outside yourself and into the landscape of another's soul. It asks something of us and challenges us to expand our understanding. And sometimes, the cost may seem too high. We may be indifferent, content with the familiar contours of our own experience.

Yet, when we yearn for authentic connection, for a shared sense of humanity, listening becomes not just an option but a necessity. In the very act of opening ourselves to the other, to their unique perspective, we deepen our understanding of the world and ourselves. We discover the richness in our diversity and the potential for growth and transformation that awaits us in the sacred space of authentic encounter.

So, the question remains for all of us: *Am I willing to open the heart's door? To listen deeply, to truly know another, and in doing so, to know myself more fully?*

NOTHING EXISTS IN ISOLATION

The open heart extends to embrace our greater identity, our place as a link, a thread, an integral part of an interconnected universe where nothing exists in isolation. In this wholeness of being, each of us lives as an essential part of a complex web of relationships, interactions, and interdependencies. Everything is contingent on everything else. All thoughts, emotions, and mental states are influenced by and connected to the world in which we live.

This interconnectedness forms the fabric of our existence.

It's empowering to recognize the far-reaching consequences of our actions and know that in our interconnected universe, our actions impact not only ourselves but also the world we live in and that we all have "skin in the game" of caring for each other.

> It's only when we truly know and understand
> that we have a limited time on earth—and that
> we have no way of knowing when our time is up—
> that we will begin to live each day to the fullest,
> as if it was the only one we had.
>
> *Elisabeth Kübler-Ross*

WHEN THE HEART CHOOSES ACTION

As we grow to understand how interconnection and awareness of our actions and choices reverberate in the lives of others, we are motivated to make more mindful decisions. Recognizing our shared humanity highlights our responsibility toward others. We can no longer separate their well-being from our own. Recognizing our ripple effect helps us to understand how helping another, even in the simplest way, can set off a chain of positive actions—and that conversely, a careless action can cause unexpected damage.

The resonance of the open heart brings empathy; we readily consider the well-being of others, actively contributing to a better society. Our commitment to a legacy of choosing kindness and helpfulness over selfishness, care over indifference, blooms as we do what we can to ensure we leave the world a little better than we found it. We find ourselves encouraged.

Recognition spurs us to small daily actions, such as smiling at a stranger, offering help to someone struggling, and supporting local initiatives that improve our neighborhood and community. Our consumption becomes more mindful as we consider ethical and environmental impacts. Our concerns broaden as we support organizations working to create positive change.

WE CAN CHANGE

Apartheid was part of my childhood evolution. The Dutch Reformed Church was then South Africa's main religion, with deep representation and dominance in the police and political arenas of power. Only by chance did my family end up in Canada rather than South Africa when we left the Netherlands.

I was raised on the words of the Children's Bible, which we read daily. Both then and now, I take the parables and stories of Jesus as truths to live by. When I learned about apartheid, the horrors imposed by my church and compatriots who ruled South Africa, it didn't make sense to me. I began to question.

The older I got, the louder and more persistent those questions became. I no longer relied on others for the truth. I did my own research and drew my own conclusions. I learned how cruelty and racism were defended and rationalized by cherry-picking from the Bible story of Noah. I read Paton's book, *Cry, the Beloved Country*, the cry for love and redemption. I continued learning about the courage and wise counsel of men like Desmond Tutu and Nelson Mandela. The more

I learned, the more I changed. My heart turned to activism, and I became at odds with the "walk" of the church. Only after Nelson Mandela's release and ensuing political and human rights unrest did the church release its grip and acknowledge the abuse of apartheid.

Desmond Tutu (1931–2021), former bishop of Johannesburg and secretary general of the South African Council of Churches (SACC), was a unifying leader in the campaign against apartheid and the 1984 Nobel Peace Prize winner. In 1986, he was appointed archbishop of Cape Town, and after the fall of apartheid, he was appointed by Nelson Mandela to the Truth and Reconciliation Commission.

Tutu's worldview can be captured in three words: *umntu ngumtu ngabantu*, which loosely translates to, "A person is a person through other people—I am because you are and you are because I am." The phrase is a poetic expression of deep empathy. It embodies the philosophy of *Ubuntu*, a concept deeply rooted in Southern African cultures, emphasizing the interconnectedness of humanity and the importance of community. The phrase speaks to the notion that our humanity is not isolated but rather formed, validated, and sustained by our interactions, connections, and contributions to the community.

Tutu often invoked this phrase to illustrate the essence of Ubuntu, highlighting the idea that our individual identities and existence are profoundly tied to our relationships with others. He used this phrase to advocate for reconciliation and unity, particularly during South Africa's transition from apartheid, believing that embracing Ubuntu could help heal the wounds of the past and build a more harmonious future by fostering understanding and cooperation among diverse communities.

Deep empathy refers to the capacity to connect with others, to welcome *you* in me, and to *feel felt* by others. It is a receptive state of mind that allows us to accept others as they are without judgment. Interpersonal attunement arises when we focus on another person to such a degree that we bring their inner world and emotional state into our awareness.

Umntu ngumtu ngabantu is also about a sense of shared responsibility. It suggests that we recognize our shared humanity by respecting, supporting, and caring for one another. By acknowledging the value of others, we affirm our own existence and place in the collective fabric of society.

> Only in terms of other people does the individual become conscious of his own being, his own duties, his privileges, and his responsibilities towards himself and towards other people. When he suffers, he does not suffer alone but with the corporate group; when he rejoices, he rejoices not alone but with his kinsmen, his neighbors and his relatives whether dead or living.
>
> *John Mbiti*

WHEN THE HEART LEADS

It's easy to feel small, ineffective, and powerless when we look at the power and wealth of our corporate world. Our government leaders can feel like they are not part of what we think of as our "normal world."

It's easy to think we have no power to change and believe that there is little we can do. It's a kind of hopelessness that is deceiving. That leads to giving up and passivity.

The world we dream of is shaped not by external forces but by boundless, uninhibited resources within each one of us. Love, kindness, compassion, wisdom—collectively, these qualities are the real movers and shakers of our world, the real influencers.

Collectively, we are tireless and unstoppable.

When geese fly in formation, they are not a group of individuals; they're a single interconnected entity, each in turn a leader and a follower. The leaders fly slightly higher, taking the brunt of the headwinds, falling back when tired, replaced by a new leader, maximizing their endurance ten, twenty, thirty-fold. They all contribute—without any thought or sense of being a leader or a follower.

Accept it or not, each one of us is a leader. Being just a follower, without power, influence, or merit, is a myth we tell ourselves.

Every minute of every day, we are modeling our leadership. We lead when we're passive, unresponsive, and unavailable to others. We lead when washing the dishes, getting our kids ready for school, and smiling at the person bagging our groceries. We lead when we do what some think of as small things. We lead when we relinquish our role, when we offer to share the lead, and when we briefly help and support.

Consciously or unconsciously, we lead by modeling. Consciously or not, we are participants in this world. Co-creators of our norms, of our culture. How we show up matters. What we show up for matters. What we say to others matters. What we do when we feel down and out matters. When we reach out to help someone else, it matters. When we don't, it matters. We, us, you, and I, are the creators of the world we inhabit. We select our leaders. Whatever power they have over us—we gave it to them.

We cannot know the impact of our actions or the influence we've had on another. Whether we like it or not, accept it or not, our actions are not isolated incidents. Give up the notion that we are small, that we can escape from responsibility.

No hero comes out of their mother's womb full-grown; each snowstorm settles one small flake at a time, and each journey begins by putting one foot in front of the other.

Moment by moment, based on your momentary potential, take your place. Be world peace. Be loving and compassionate. Be aware. Be inner peace. Be wise. Be inspiration. Be your ideal.

Know that you are not one but a multitude, a co-creator, an influencer. And know that you can act from that wisdom—because it's heart wisdom—and it is your deepest, truest self.

IF THE HEART COULD DREAM

If the heart could dream, perhaps it would envision a world overflowing with love, kindness, and profound connections, a world that resonates with compassion and grace. A world where healing and forgiveness thrive, where past wounds are mended, and empathy fosters reconciliation.

Perhaps it would dream of a world where compassion transcends barriers of race, religion, or ideology. Where every heartbeat signifies not just life, but a rhythm of understanding, acceptance, and forgiveness.

In its dream, the heart might relish moments of pure joy, forging experiences that resonate deeply—moments filled with laughter, love, and a profound sense of fulfillment. And a reality where people pursue their passions wholeheartedly, embracing their true selves without fear or judgment.

If the heart could dream, it might dream that we'd finally free ourselves from the notion of a fixed, objective reality, understanding instead that change is inevitable, and that transformation would not be possible without change. Freed from attachments and unquenchable desire, spontaneity and authenticity would arise without effort.

In the heart's dream, it may imagine a time when humanity thoroughly understood the fluid nature of all things, including our own identity, even our very existence. Where we embrace, rather than fear, the ambiguity of reality. A world where we experience the wonder of our interconnectedness and see the beauty of life's uncertainty and ever-changing nature.

Or perhaps, if the heart could dream, it would dream of what Thich Nhat Hanh called *interbeing*, morphing from form to form—this moment, a bird soaring the skies; the next moment, a dolphin leaping and spinning, clicking and whistling, and landing with a big splash. Or perhaps the heart would dream it was a humble butterfly, relishing its existence in a thoroughly interconnected universe.

Last night, I dreamed I was a butterfly, flitting from flower to flower, flitting from plant to plant. Or is it now that I am a butterfly dreaming I am Chuang Tzu, flitting from sentence to sentence, flitting from word to word?

Chuang Tzu

Heart Questions

1. What new heart questions are arising for you at this point in your life?

2. What dreams would your heart most welcome?

3. How might you begin to tend to the dreams of your heart?

Chapter 14

Embodying Your Heart Wisdom

The people are a story that never ends, a river
that winds and falls and gleams erect in many
dawns; lost in deep gulleys, it turns to dust,
rushes in the spring freshet, emerges to the sea.

Meridel Le Sueur

———

MY FATHER HAD this way of . . . well, of seeing. Not just with his eyes, but with something deeper. A kind of . . . gnosis. He would look away, "inside," and often reference an inner space, that space "between river and land," as I discussed in chapter 10.

Dad wasn't just talking about the physical world, of course. He was talking about the *heart*. The human heart, with its capacity for both stability and change, for both grounded-ness and fluidity. We contain multitudes, as Whitman said. We *are* the river and the land, constantly shifting, constantly evolving, yet always anchored to something . . . essential.

He'd watch the fishermen on the river, these small boats bobbing on the surface. And he'd say, "The longer you look, the more you see." It's not just about what's visible, he'd explain. It's about the effort, the persistence, the *depth* of your gaze. The same was true of the land. My brothers, they became contractors—moving mountains, literally. I saw firsthand how much effort went into shaping the earth, digging deep beneath the surface. My father contrasted this with "water spiders" that skim across the top, unable or not called to delve deeper. Not judging, mind you. Just . . . observing. Noting the different ways we interact with the world, with reality itself.

And then there was the question of dialogue. He noticed how some people truly engaged in conversation, a genuine exchange of ideas, a *dance* of speaking and listening. Others, he'd say, they just monologue. They broadcast. They don't truly *hear*. This relates back to the river and the land—are we flowing and receptive like the river, or fixed and unyielding like the land?

Finally, Dad spoke of expansion. I believe he was thinking of the community we lived in. Some people, he pointed out, stay close to the "core of emergence," confined and restricted in their thinking and experiences. Others, like explorers venturing between the river and the land, embrace a broader range of possibilities, traveling both outward into the world and inward into themselves. They understand that true growth lies in navigating the space between these apparent opposites and in recognizing the interconnectedness of all things. His "between river and land" wasn't just a description of a landscape; it was a map for living a full and meaningful life.

HOW SHALL WE STAND?

Life today is life in crisis. As in a war zone, dailiness is fractured with change, the shattering of old certainties. We live in dark clouds of danger, our fear of the unknown.

When and where do we all stand there? Can we stand as we live in this era of uncertainty? The discerning quality of the heart is called on to weigh options, to find the wisest response, taking everything into account.

The door of the heart opens and closes to our lived lives. In the flow of life's complexity, we are empowered to choose and do our best to weigh what is needed and what is right for the given moments.

We live in a time of shattered certainties. The sky of the future no longer offers promises or the mirage of control. The seductive assurance of certainty no longer gentles our anxiety. The real question today is, "Where can we stand in all this inescapable knowing of our *not knowing*?"

Where do we find our footing amidst this uncertainty? Can we even stand firm in such an era? Our hearts are called upon to discern, to weigh options with wisdom, considering all that is at stake.

Now, we dare not splinter who we are. All that we are is needed: the mind, the heart, the fear, the hope, the joy, the sorrow, the known, and especially our awareness of the unknown.

This deep, contemplative process, this discerning capacity for listening, is not appeased by easy answers but listening to what calls on us—the courage to live in the questions, to trust our heart's compass, even when the map is unclear.

We do what we can, where we can. Not in the crescendos of great system-shattering explosions but in the small candlelight of what we can do where we are with what we have.

BALANCE AND THE HEART

We talk about balance a lot: physical balance, emotional balance, and spiritual balance. I have been quick to speak of balance, but I'm discovering that it's not as simple as it can sound. In the months before this book finally came together, I had a humbling experience playing soccer with two-year-olds (don't ask!) and ended up in the hospital and rehab with a multi-fractured hip and a broken wrist.

This is life. It changed things. I tend to be in my head more than my body, but when I fell, my body pulled me out of my head, out of my proclivity to abstractions.

During that journey of injury and healing something profound happened. Physical therapy became a kind of . . . spiritual practice. I realized, viscerally, how deeply connected my physical balance was to my mental and emotional state. It wasn't just about working with my physical therapist on figuring out the mechanics of standing on one leg or learning to walk up the stairs again, it became about a deeper understanding of the *union* of mind and body. It was about an authentic coming together of the two. I was challenged to be present, fully embodied, in a way I hadn't understood before.

To regain my physical balance, I had to be present and aware in a deeper way.

That led me to consider how life balance can also be lost. I live (am sometimes lost) in my head, caught in my life narratives. Unaware, not present, not consciously living in my body. I started experimenting, trying to feel the difference between that one-dimensional awareness and then expanding to include my body and the more fantastic world around me. Now I understand that concentration, single-pointed mindfulness, is a helpful and important skill. But I was being pointed to something more. One day I realized that it could lead to neglect, to lack of consideration.

What I learned is that balance is not automatic. It happens as moment-by-moment practice, and like breathing, I had to keep coming back to it.

It made me think of role-taking, how we must learn and then return to putting ourselves in another's shoes to see the world through their eyes as well as our own. It's easy to get so caught up in our thoughts and feelings that we forget to consider others. It's not just about the mind and body but also about balancing our own needs and perspectives with those of others.

When the body and mind are in harmony, we can meet someone else, attune to someone else in more subtle ways. Self-absorbed awareness dissolves to meet in a union of both self and other.

The open heart now naturally flows beyond its own ego boundaries. Engages as a child might, into the spontaneous dance of relationship.

I see how it is. It is a practice, a discipline, a continual letting go of the self.

ENCOUNTERING THE VOID

In the delicate balance between self and other, we encounter the void. Some of us, lost in the abyss of our own woundedness, become fixated on the emptiness within. Others, fearing that void, cling to the illusion of a separate self, building walls of defensiveness and control.

Both extremes become forms of imprisonment. Both lead to a contraction of the heart, a diminishment of love. True freedom, true love, lies in the embrace of both self and other, in the recognition of our interconnectedness.

The heart, it seems, is drawn to both the void and the vibrant world around it. Some of us, like moths to a flame, are drawn to the mystery of invisible inner depths, to the quiet emptiness within. Others, like sunflowers turning toward the sun, find nourishment in the external world, in the bustling marketplace of human interaction. Both are needed.

I recall a conversation with a spiritual director, wise in the ways of the Enneagram, who described this duality with remarkable clarity. "Some people," she said, "live right next door to the void. It's a magnet for them, a constant source of fascination and exploration. Others are more captivated by the external environment, by the endless possibilities for connection and engagement."

She likened the void dwellers to those who stay close to the hearth, seeking solace in the inner depths, while the environment seekers are forever out in the neighborhood, chatting with neighbors, exploring new avenues of interaction. Their energy, she observed, is like a garden hose spraying outward, seeking connection through expression and engagement.

"But," she cautioned, "their connection is limited. They need someone to receive their outpourings, to listen and respond. They are not always adept at the reciprocal dance of true connection."

I, myself, am drawn to the void, to the silent depths where the heart can commune with the Mystery. I find energy in connecting with others who share this affinity, who are comfortable dwelling in the liminal spaces. It is like being drawn to the event horizon of a black hole, a place of immense gravity and profound stillness.

And yet, I also recognize the importance of the external world, of the vibrant tapestry of human relationships. I see myself as a connector, bringing people together, facilitating their interactions, and then stepping back to observe the fruits of their connection. It is a draining process, this participation in the world, but also deeply fulfilling.

EMBRACING THE DANCE OF UNCERTAINTY

Perhaps, I mused, the existentialist philosophers were drawn to the void? Were they compelled by the horrors of war and the fragility of human existence to confront the ultimate questions of meaning and purpose? Perhaps their flocking together was a way to make sense of the darkness, to find solace in shared reflection. Camus, one of those writers, reminds us that in the end, we need to consider how to live with what we come to understand as reality.

And so, we return to the heart, to its capacity to embrace both the abyss and the world, both certainty and uncertainty. Some of us, drawn to the depths, grapple with existential questions about the mysteries of existence. Others are more comfortable in the realm of the known, in certainty, in the illusion of control. But life, in its wisdom, often disrupts our carefully constructed paradigms. We are confronted with uncertainty, with the limits of our knowledge. And in those moments, we have a choice: to cling to our old ways of knowing, or to surrender to the unknown, to embrace the dance of uncertainty.

For it is in the space between certainty and uncertainty, in the liminal realm where the heart can both know and not know, that true wisdom resides. It is a space of vulnerability, of openness, of radical acceptance. And it is here, in this delicate balance, that we find the freedom to truly love, to truly live.

THE INTEGRATED SPIRITUAL JOURNEY

Our inner lives can become too self-centered. Our inner landscape can be a place of extraordinary discovery and deep insight, but it can also be a trap. We can become self-absorbed, lost in our inner terrain, and lose sight of others.

The integrated, mature spiritual journey is not just about the self; it's about connection, compassion, and love.

It's about recognizing the divine in everyone and everything, even in those we ferociously disagree with.

On the developmental journey of movement, flow, we "meet," master, integrate, and transcend. We don't burn down what we leave behind as we deepen or rise above. Nothing is lost. The earlier levels are not lost!

For example, in the last few years, I have been watching the three little girls who are my neighbors. Their first movements in infancy become advanced motor skills as they integrate coordination and balance. They soon ride bicycles, skate, and dance. Each little girl is different from the other, all stages interconnected, progression both linear and not linear in the back-and-forth dance of progression and integration.

Hierarchical development can take different forms. We can depict it as a ladder we climb that allows us to ascend and see more. We can think of it as a river, widening, deepening, yet still carrying the essence of its source. Even now, in my eighth decade, I can drop to the floor and crawl if the spirit moves me. The infant's movement is not forgotten; it's woven into the tapestry of who I am.

My young neighbors each unfold in their own way. Linear progression in part, but also a dance of integration, a back-and-forth, a constant interplay of what was, what is, and what will be. The clumsy stumble informs the elegant pirouette. It's all there, held within the expanding circle of their being.

It's all a dance, a constant balancing act between the inner and the outer, the self and the other, the void and the world. Even positive things, like introspection or exploring "the void," can leave us so lost in ourselves that we lose sight of the world and the people in it. It's a constant process of learning and adjusting.

And the grace, I think, is in the falling, in the humbling moments that remind us that we're all in this together.

AS YOU CLOSE THIS BOOK

Since childhood, I've carried a deep and abiding ache, a felt awareness of injustice, of moral injury in the world. It's an awareness, not only of systemic disregard and "care-lessness" but of my own complicity in the brokenness of the world. I believe it's a burden that many sensitive, empathetic hearts feel and share. It's an ache in the heart that speaks to a fundamental tension within us, between the world as it *is* and the world as we believe it could be, long for it to be. And I've always had an aversion to walking away, to finding exemption from responsibility, to protecting the defenses that veil or shroud that knowing.

Perhaps it was born of early encounters with war and the harsh realities of life—of hunger, awareness of the camps, of bombs, of the fate of soldiers, of losing extended family, friends, language, of witnessing the anguish of my immigrant parents. Perhaps my heartache came later from seeing the moral injustices, the environmental degradation, all the times when we turn inward, away from each other, to protect ourselves. Defenses leave us with inner fractures, places where wholeness feels compromised.

I feel privileged to have witnessed fierce resistance to "things that are wrong" in my childhood. Perhaps that instilled an injunction not to back away, but to go *toward*. It left me with grief, anger, and sadness—difficult emotions evoked by suffering that I did not want to intellectualize or rationalize away. I discovered that to embrace these feelings might be a path to healing, understanding, even wisdom. And I have been surprised by joy, by contentment, by deep gratitude.

In my Christian upbringing, I was tutored to walk the life that Jesus exemplified. My heart followed the way of Jesus as true but did not take in the conviction that there was only one path to "light." Later, in Buddhist practice, I took the Bodhisattva vow, a vast and compassionate commitment to a dream—a dream that speaks to the yearning within us for a world free from suffering. Like walking the way of Jesus, this vow can feel overwhelming as I face my own limitations. Yet even though I often fail to show up, I return to that intention and commitment, to offer kindness and healing in my limited, broken-hearted way.

I have sometimes found a way to action, to places where I could make a difference. But we also live with enormous barriers of cultural and systemic influences that shape individual choices and make ethical living a constant uphill battle. I've found that supporting those who work for change becomes an act of solidarity, a way of weaving our individual efforts into a larger tapestry of hope. Change must be systemic *as well as* personal. The work must be on both fronts.

I hope this book may contribute in some meaningful way. I hope that the stories and thoughts, the struggles, may offer to you a flicker of recognition, a moment of encouragement for your work, of solace or insight when the road is dark.

The complexities of life, life as I have lived it, have offered a journey of continuous learning and growth. Life is a process of holding complexities with an open heart. It offers us chances to acknowledge the pain and grief of our brokenness without becoming consumed. Life allows us, time after time, to come back to remembering our interconnectedness with each other and all the other inhabitants of this wondrous planet.

I hope that sharing my own journey has resonated, provided support for *your* journey, and served as a reminder that you are not alone, that *we are not alone* in our shared human experience. That honesty and authenticity are gifts. And that what *you* do, even your smallest acts of compassion, can send ripples outward. That we can dream together, work together, toward a time when the ideal will become real.

I leave you with more heart questions, ones I continue to ask myself, ones whose answers may vary on any given day:

What are your deepest questions? Of yourself? Of others? Of the world? Of truth as you know it? What energizes you to action, to agency? Where do you find rest, support? Where do you feel that you must act, that you "can do no other?" Where do you shut down? Where are you in balance? When you fall, where can you find help? What do you forget, and what helps you to remember? And what can you give? Where can you heal? Where can you mend? Where and with whom can you be playful? Where can you just be and do nothing? Where can you comfort and bring healing?

> The most beautiful thing in the world
> is a heart that is changing.
>
> *Lara Ackerman*

Joyful Appreciation for a Lovely Friend

THIS BOOK IS about the power of connections and the trauma of disconnections. It's about caring for the common good. It was inspired by my dear friend Joyce McFarland. When I met Joyce about three decades ago, I was immediately drawn into the communal web of connections she'd fostered over the years—gently, doggedly nurturing the weak, deploying the strong, and expanding, constantly expanding the reach.

Joyce was a master connector. She was undaunted by the difficulty or effort required to birth both local and far-reaching connections and then work to galvanize them into fruition. To her community in Minneapolis, she shared her energy and resources freely and generously. More times than I can recount, I was awed by her tireless dedication to the common good of all life. She could be as fierce as a force of nature or as gentle as summer rain. And it was a great joy to watch.

Connectors like Joyce have a vision and an intuitive sense of where, how, and who needs to be connected to this organization or that community action. Endowed with a bone-deep faith and an unwavering devotion to the common good, they harness resources and deploy them wisely. They are able to galvanize others to stand together, to dream the impossible, and to work relentlessly to bring it into reality. They make a difference, and Joyce made a difference. She acted to give voice to the muted, to empower the disempowered, and to clear the way for those whose lives had been thwarted and opportunity denied.

She did not do it alone, of course. She knew how easily overwhelmed we can become when we stand alone. But when we have each other's backs and stand together, we become a force not easily undone. Her husband and partner, Dick, always had her back, and she his. Together they created the McFarland Family Fund and through it charmed hundreds of volunteers and donors into opening their hearts and wallets for the sake of others who were less fortunate.

Once, in a kitchen table conversation we had some years ago about community action, she bent down, reaching for an electrical cord lying on the floor near our feet. "This is how you do it," she said, "You must plug in if you want to be a part of something, if you want to make something happen."

Over the years, I often ran into her on one street or another, shopping bags hanging from both her arms—filled with cards, books, miniature works of art, and a myriad of other purchases she'd made that day to support a cause, a person, a church, or a mission. Then hours were spent penning inspiring calligraphic messages, making phone calls, attending meetings, shepherding, and scaffolding, turning hope into action and action into fruition—so much so that she often needed a gentle reminder to pause, to unplug, to retreat into her private wellspring of stillness and deeply reflective mind, take a moment to allow her natural introverted nature to gather and restore itself.

And Joyce was also an artist. She had a keen eye for the beauty that shone from within. Her calligraphy was like that. Even her garden was like that. She made everything she did appear effortless like she was born to it. Perhaps she was.

Having an eye for beauty and mastery, she recognized it in others, like Parker J. Palmer. When she met him, she became enchanted with his work. She sensed the same deep, instinctual passion for the common good that resided within herself. Joyce resonated deeply with the hard inner work Parker Palmer called his readers to. Like herself, he intuitively knew how to gather and return what was broken to wholeness.

So, true to form, Joyce put her weight behind Palmer's work, especially in his role as founder of the Center for Courage & Renewal, and devoted herself to supporting his mission. In appreciation, she and Dick were honored for their support in a film documenting Parker Palmer's work. That was early in 2022.

Only a few months later, my dear friend, whom I greatly miss, died after suffering a stroke. It was a significant loss to all who knew her. It is a great fortune that in the wake of her abundant life, a thriving web of connection will continue her work.

Forever inspired by her memory, ignited by her spirit, and with her presence still reverberating in my heart, this book is dedicated to her legacy.

Gratitudes

THIS BOOK FOUND life in fits and starts, as a testament to interdependence, a product of nagging questions and choices, voices heeded and renounced, overlooked. I am deeply grateful for teachers, challenging conversations, lectures, writings, for living in a time in history where I had access to diverse traditions and philosophies.

I acknowledge the immense privilege of having the space, time, and freedom to discover, reflect, work, study, write—rare gifts I don't take lightly.

To my clients, unnamed but known in your hearts, who shared your journeys and deepened my understanding, know that in our mutual discovery, you profoundly shaped mine.

On the practical side, bringing this book to life called for expertise far beyond my own. My deepest gratitude flows to Wanda Isle, whose wisdom, unwavering encouragement, and skillful writing and editing transformed my early musings into a coherent, living whole.

My heartfelt thanks extend to the dear friends who read and encouraged throughout the fits and starts of this journey: Marilyn Kaman, Anne Buchanan, Bill Monson, Deb Haddock, Lisa Schuurman, Lianna Reitsma, Erin Burkett Meyer, Steve Miles, Brenda Hartman, Gail Rosenblum. Julie Andrus, Mark Gemmel, and Tim Burkett—I know what you did. Thank you! To others whose names I have not mentioned here, please know your contributions are held in my heart.

A deep bow of gratitude to Parker J. Palmer. Parker, your encouragement and generous foreword was the wind beneath the wings of this book. When the time came to find a publisher, it was Parker who connected me with Shelly Francis, a kindred spirit—author, editor, and publisher. Shelly, I do not know how to thank you! It was your boundless personal support, quiet patience, and awesome professional expertise that shepherded these pages into print.

My deepest respect, love, and appreciation to my still-living sister, Nelly, and to the late members of my beloved family. And, to my father and all, who like him, lend their hearts' courage to protect the common good and freedom for all sentient beings.

Nelly was born in 1930 as fascism was rising. I'd like to share her recent words to invoke the personal and collective courage of all who read this book: "It feels as if my life is between bookends of authoritarianism. We need our good hearts now, our brave and willing hearts."

About the Author

LENI DE MIK, PhD, is a clinical psychologist with a remarkable journey spanning continents and challenges. Born in Nazi-occupied Netherlands in 1941, she survived wartime hardship and immigration, experiences that shaped her profound understanding of human resilience. With over 40 years of clinical practice, Leni has worked as a teacher, activist, author, and therapist. Rooted in her Christian Calvinist upbringing but deeply influenced by Zen and Tibetan Buddhist traditions, Leni was among the first certified to teach Cultivating Emotional Balance—a secular program emerging from dialogues between His Holiness the Dalai Lama and leading behavioral scientists. Dr. de Mik lives in Minneapolis, continuing to explore the depths of human compassion.

About Creative Courage Press

CREATIVE COURAGE PRESS is a small, independent publishing company founded in 2020 by Shelly L. Francis, inspired by the people she met while writing *The Courage Way: Leading and Living with Integrity* (Berrett-Koehler, 2018). Now, in collaboration with other authors, we are creating courage for the complexity of being human.

Get to know the essential voices of our remarkable authors and their refreshing ideas for leading change from the heart. Together we hope to generate meaningful conversations in our communities.

Visit us online to get fortified with resources and reflections for creating your own courageous way of life. As we grow, we invite you to grow with us.

www.CreativeCouragePress.com
hello@CreativeCouragePress.com

**CREATIVE
COURAGE
PRESS**

www.ingramcontent.com/pod-product-compliance
Lightning Source LLC
Chambersburg PA
CBHW021709120626
46545CB00004B/1482